Swiss Made

New Architecture from Switzerland

Steven Spier
with Martin Tschanz

Photographs by
Christian Richters

With 351 illustrations, 262 in colour

Thames & Hudson

Contents

006 'Innovation and the Patient Search',
Steven Spier

014 Bearth + Deplazes
016 Chairlift Station, Arosa, Graubünden
020 House Meuli, Fläsch, Graubünden
026 Ice-rink conversion, Arosa, Graubünden
028 Contemporary Art Gallery, Marktoberdorf,
Germany

032 Burkhalter Sumi Architekten
034 EMPA renovation, Dübendorf, Zurich
038 Multi-Family Villas, Witikon, Zurich
046 Office Centre, Opfikon, Zurich
048 Sulzer Building renovation, Winterthur

054 Gion A. Caminada
056 Stalls and Abattoir, Vrin, Graubünden
058 Totenstube, Vrin, Graubünden
064 Single-family house, Vignon, Graubünden
068 Hotel Alpina, Vals, Graubünden

074 Jürg Conzett
076 Surasuns Footbridge, Viamala, Graubünden
082 Pedestrian Bridge, Bruges, Belgium
086 Footbridge, Viamala, Graubünden

088 Diener & Diener
090 Java Island housing, Amsterdam, the
Netherlands
094 ABB Power Tower, Baden
100 Commercial centre, Lucerne
104 Swiss Embassy, Berlin, Germany

112 Gigon & Guyer
114 Liner Museum, Appenzell
122 Susenbergstrasse apartment buildings, Zurich
126 Kalkriese Archaeological Museum Park,
Osnabrück, Germany
130 Pflegiareal housing and offices, Zurich

134 <u>Marcel Meili, Markus Peter Architekten</u>
136 RiffRaff 2, Zurich
142 Swiss Re Rüschlikon Centre for Global
    Dialogue, Zurich
148 Parasite House, Rotterdam, the Netherlands
152 Swiss Embassy, Washington, DC, USA

154 <u>Peter Märkli</u>
156 La Congiunta, Giornico, Ticino
160 Single-family house, Hünenberg
166 School, Zurich North
168 Single-family house, Azmoos

172 <u>Miller & Maranta</u>
174 Market hall, Aarau
178 Schwarzpark apartments, Basel
180 Volta Schoolhouse, Basel

188 <u>Morger & Degelo Architekten</u>
190 Liechtenstein Art Museum, Vaduz
194 St. Alban-Ring housing, Basel
196 House Müller, Staufen, Basel
200 Reinach town centre, Basel

202 <u>Valerio Olgiati</u>
204 Schoolhouse, Paspels, Graubünden
210 Yellow House, Flims, Graubünden
214 Office building, Zurich

216 <u>Peter Zumthor</u>
218 Sound Box, Hanover Expo 2000, Germany
224 Topography of Terror, Berlin, Germany
226 Single-family house, Graubünden
230 Kunsthaus, Bregenz, Austria

236 'Essentially Realism', Martin Tschanz
244 Architect biographies
246 Project credits
252 Bibliography
255 Photography credits
256 Copyright page

Swiss Made

'Innovation and the Patient Search'

Minimalism, neo-modernism, the new simplicity, the *neue Sachlichkeit*, the box. These are all terms used to describe contemporary Swiss architecture. They undoubtedly all have some truth in them. Even a casual observer can discern a reduction in form and a preference for the orthogonal, a very high standard of construction, precise detailing. One can even admit at least some connection to minimal art. But formal and visual similarities in themselves are not very interesting. (The architecture is sometimes sophomorically accused of being boring.) The issue, rather, is: how has an important architecture developed that has been so influential for the last ten years and at the same time is distinctive from developments elsewhere?

Before resorting to clichés about national character, I would point to the crux to understanding Swiss architecture: it is perhaps unique in the developed world for its continuous development of a tradition. And that tradition has become its own breed of modernism. The romantic populism of chalet architecture and mountain villages notwithstanding, the culture of modernism is so pervasive in Switzerland that it need not even be articulated, much less defended. It is the culture within which every architect, planner, graphic designer, client and building tradesman operates. It is the unquestioned basis on which the built environment is constructed.

Switzerland industrialized late, the necessary political conditions having been created only with the constitution of 1848, but then did so with characteristic efficiency. It was similarly late coming to modernism but did so emphatically in 1924 in Basel with the formation of the left-wing ABC group by El Lissitzky and Mart Stam that included Emil Roth, Hans Schmidt, Hannes Meyer and Hans Wittwer. It wanted architecture replaced by design, which would encompass urban planning, building technology, architecture and the very organization of daily life. Design would be led by scientific principles. Uncharacteristically strident for Switzerland, it was

typically moderated. This is a national characteristic: everything is negotiable. (In 1936 the preservationists and the advocates of modernism actually signed a document pledging support for each other.) A softer, less ideological approach is exemplified in Alfred Roth's influential *The New Architecture* (1940). An anthology, it avoided the questions of ideology and construction and instead placed emphasis on well-programmed, well-detailed buildings in a restrained, even elegant modern aesthetic.

The effort to be modern while accommodating regional traditions and concerns advanced to international acclaim in the 1940s and 1950s. The emphasis continued to be on good planning and quality construction within a restrained modern vocabulary. It is perhaps easy to mock this pragmatism, and periodically the Swiss themselves feel insufficiently engaged in the developed world's bouts of heedless idealism, but it has proven decisive in removing that tiresome dispute between the avant-garde and tradition. The pendulum between the polite modernism of *Sachliches Bauen* and a more vociferous variety did swing back and forth, but the latter was always subsumed into something Swiss, where changes in direction require the careful building of consensus and are incremental. This is true in all spheres of public life. That it takes a long time for anything to change is frustrating but the eventual quality is gratifying. The great benefit of such a culture architecturally is that practice can advance on what went before. This maturity means there is a certain quiet humility to the way one goes about things; there are few *enfants terribles*. It means that architects are actually working to the Corbusian principles of a *recherche architecturale* and a 'patient search'. In a media- and fame-obsessed, ever more frenzied world these are remarkable traits. The architecture culture is thus highly evolved. Observations and critiques from within it recognize strong differences among examples of the current work and describe those in sophisticated terms.

One of the many things that has made this patient search possible is that Swiss cities did not suffer the vast destruction during the Second World War that other European cities did. The country was therefore not confronted with the need to rebuild nor to rethink things on a massive scale. Rotterdam had to be almost entirely rebuilt, as did large parts of British, Belgian, French and eastern European cities, to name but a few. Germany had to rebuild not only its cities but also its culture. The physical and social destruction of the war gave impetus to the modernist project, as did later the development of competing communist and capitalist world views and a staggering prosperity in the developed world. The response architecturally and urbanistically seems astonishing now in its confidence. An affection for the avant-garde returns regularly, almost nostalgically, to the big idea, the big form, the bold move. Switzerland, in its usual fashion, stood slightly outside these developments without rejecting them. For its slate has never been wiped clean. It may have fewer postwar masterpieces than many European countries, but it also has fewer egregious mistakes.

As coarse a rendition of Swiss modernism as the present one necessarily has to be, the larger point is that contemporary architecture in Switzerland has developed within a mature, modernist tradition and a culture that has so far allowed architects to get on with building. And architecture is unmistakably understood as building. That this is not tautological shows only how radically the profession elsewhere has changed. In Switzerland it noted and considered but did not engage theatrically with the theoretical speculations of the last twenty years – historicism, post-structuralism, deconstruction and now the blob. When the architects in this book were developing their practices they were looking not to the United States or Great Britain but to Spain, Portugal and Italy, to people who were quietly developing an architecture in a modern idiom for a postmodern era. They were not teaching in order to support their practices, as were their counterparts in many other countries. They were too busy entering competitions and building. The theoretical discourse in Switzerland never strays too far from building, nor does the education at the Federal Institute of Technology (Eidgenössische Technische Hochschule, ETH). (In the worst case, the architecture proceeds without any

guiding concept and so is merely a set of finely crafted details.) It can even be said that it is not the quality of the idea but the quality of the thing itself that is important. The culture is uninterested in intellectuals, suspicious of the big idea. The architects in this book are conscious of working at the end of a culture that expects that things will be well built and still has the construction skills to accomplish that. Much of this work is possible only because the architect can build things that in other countries are not even capable of consideration.[1] There is a general feeling among Swiss architects that the profession in Europe is slowly being destroyed under the influence of American models, where the responsibilities of and opportunities for the architect are so diminished.

Ironically, the centrality of building had its most recent confirmation in the events of 1968. In Switzerland, as elsewhere, the social relevance of architecture was found wanting and architectural education increasingly turned to disciplines such as sociology, anthropology and behavioural and political science. The earlier glee at the idea that modernism might become teachable had degenerated into desiccation, systems and design methods. Architecture itself – space, place, tectonics – had become marginalized but was dramatically reasserted during the two-year visiting professorship at ETH Zurich of Aldo Rossi between 1972 and 1974. Along with young architects from the Italian-speaking canton of Ticino, he argued that architecture was actually an autonomous discipline with its own history, theory, tasks and worth. This was as difficult at the time for his fellow professors as it was exhilarating for the students. He was joined importantly by Bruno Reichlin and Martin Steinmann, who called for 'the enjoyment of architecture'. The 'autonomy of architecture' sounds worryingly formal, but actually placed the complexity of architecture at the heart of our human drama. It resulted in little historicist pastiche, thanks to the ingrained modernist sensibility, and confronted Swiss architecture with the complexities of history and the city.

The *Tendenza*, which concurrently came out of Ticino in the 1970s and 1980s to achieve worldwide recognition, grappled with reconciling modernist traditions and the region's own history and culture. But the pervasive classicism of Italy from which Rossi and the rationalist movement started had little precedent north of the Alps. The centrality of architecture, however, was also a premise in the consideration of the postwar city in *Learning from Las Vegas* by Venturi et al. (1972). Its influence was promulgated by the editorship and scholarship of Stanislaus van Moos, professor of architectural history at the University of Zurich. Venturi's interest in pop culture, however, was quickly marginalized in favour of his interest in the banal; his populism was supplanted by the everyday. There was a recognition, especially from Fabio Reinhard, that the everyday north of the Alps could be found in the workaday industrial buildings of the nineteenth century and the untidiness of the urban edge. At ETH Zurich Miroslav Sik developed what he called *Analoge Architektur*, a kind of Swiss variant on the work of Venturi, Ed Ruscha and others who 'like boring things'. But its droll quality was transformed into a melancholic poesy. At the same time the history and theory department at ETH Zurich started publishing monographs on the first and second generation of Swiss modernists, which made even clearer certain characteristics of its own tradition.

This incredible theoretical ferment, which happened in such a short period, both confirmed the tenets of Swiss modernism and broadened them with more cosmopolitan issues. In rediscovering Max Bill in the 1990s and asserting him as part of a minimal tradition,[2] Switzerland was recognizing its particular history and blending of theories. Though he had long been known as a painter, sculptor, industrial designer, teacher and proponent of concrete art, the plainness or normalcy of his architecture was seen as if for the first time. Its conceptual economy and precision of execution are indeed important qualities of Swiss architecture today. While Bill was being rediscovered so were Alison and Peter Smithson, founders of Team X, who strove to understand architecture's social meaning in a postwar culture and whose designs were often radical and direct. Of particular importance was their book, *Without Rhetoric: An Architectural Aesthetic 1955–1972* (1973), which argued that in a culture that is assuredly modern one no longer needs to be strident. The architect should start from where we live, which is a state of modernity, however unheroic.

Grouping architects by country is convenient and of course there are similar characteristics to the work in this book. As I try to show, the architects are products of a particular modernist culture, which allows them room to exercise their profession. They are generally of similar ages and the product of similar times. Most were educated at ETH Zurich, which epitomizes much about Swiss culture. It is very selective, the curriculum is rigorous and it is sure where it is heading. Most importantly, it produces students of an extremely high competence and doesn't entertain the maverick sensibility. This is all true, but the present book shows how this can go awry, with interesting, sometimes amazing results. The Swiss are imbued with discretion and humility and frown upon arrogance and vanity, but none of this betokens a lack of ambition. Peter Zumthor, for instance, a world-class architect in anyone's estimation, still works and lives in a mountain village outside the provincial city of Chur.

While Zumthor was assiduously and quietly designing stunning buildings, Herzog & de Meuron were rushing to worldwide prominence and have played an important role in the public success of Swiss architecture. Jacques Herzog and Pierre de Meuron have known each other since they were children, graduating together from ETH in Zurich in 1976 and opening their office two years later. The other partners, Harry Gugger and Christine Binswanger, also grew up in Switzerland and graduated from ETH. Although they are all products of the very Swiss culture described in this introduction, and their work could only have developed from within it, they are impatient with most of that heritage. Their manner, artfulness, agility and stature do set them apart, and they were awarded the Pritzker Prize in 2001.

Public renown for Herzog & de Meuron came with Tate Modern in London (1994–98), their transformation of a

A topographic map of Switzerland.

Gigon & Guyer, The Kirchner Museum, Davos, 1990–92. A probing investigation into the material qualities of glass.

Diener & Diener, office and shops at Barfüsserplatz, Basel, 1993–95. Fitting into and challenging the European city.

Mario Botta, Casa Rotonda, Ticino, 1980–82. The pure geometries and formal explorations that brought Botta renown.

Herzog & de Meuron, apartment buildings on rue des Suisses, Paris, 1996–2000. A homogeneous and variable façade.

Peter Zumthor, protective housing for archaeological excavations, Chur, 1985–86. An early example of the reduction and precision of his work.

Herzog & de Meuron, Senior Technical School library, Eberswalde, Germany, 1993–96. Alternating bands of windows and pre-cast concrete imprinted with images chosen by German artist Thomas Ruff.

The 23 cantons of Switzerland.

Robert Maillart (1872–1940).
A typically elegant concrete bridge
by the engineer.

Santiago Calatrava, Stadelhofen
train station, Zurich, 1983–90. The
plasticity of form and expressive
structure of the underground
shopping area.

Luigi Snozzi, House
Kalmann, Ticino, 1974–76.
The Tendenza's combination
of typology and modernism.

p. 6: Herzog & de Meuron,
central signal box, Basel, 1997.
The architects' second signal
box in Basel.

Burkhalter Sumi Architekten, forestry
stations, Turbenthal, Zurich, 1991–93.
Built research into the tectonics and
construction of timber.

Peter Zumthor, Caplutta Sogn
Benedetg, Sumvitg, Graubünden,
1985–88. A temporary chapel
for a Romansch-speaking village.

huge disused power station into a modern-art museum, the commission for which they won in an international competition. It is characteristically precise and bold. However, in their earlier work, while accepting the rectangle as the predominant form, they were already experimenting radically with materials and processes, looking for hidden or lost meanings. The Ricola warehouse in Laufen (1986–87, see pp. 4–5) used banal materials for a banal programme but in such a way that the building became sensual and sculptural. Their interest in a building's skin characterizes their earlier work and is driven by an engagement with contemporary culture and by issues of perception. In the second Ricola warehouse (Mulhouse, 1992–93) the polycarbonate cladding provides the building with varied degrees of transparency depending on the light; and the images screen-printed on to these sheets give the surface a further ambiguity between textile, graphic surface and primitive sign. This last interest is pursued again in the library at Eberswalde (1993–96). An increasing interest in form and surface can be seen in the difference between the signal box 4 Auf dem Wolf (Basel, 1992–95) and the central signal box (Basel, 1994–97). Both are six-storey buildings wrapped in copper to protect the interior's electronic equipment from external disturbance, which gives the buildings an ambiguous appearance and scale. The copper ribbons are twisted as needed to admit daylight but in the central signal box, this seems to distort the form. Herzog & de Meuron's later work is even more plastic, investigating how buildings can radically transform themselves depending on their use or time of day or climate. The Roche Pharma building in Basel (1993–2000), for instance, is both a crisp glass box and a soft, seemingly billowing form; and the apartment building on rue des Suisses in Paris (1996–2000) attains varying degrees of plasticity through its shutters.

The most striking characteristic of Herzog & de Meuron's work is their boundless and intrepid curiosity. They insist that they are interested only in the direct physical and emotional impact of a building, and are constantly researching new building and material techniques to bring contemporary life to architecture. This is the reason they are more interested in the fine arts than in architecture; they find the former more critical, more radical, quicker to respond to a fast-changing world. Herzog & de Meuron have a long history of working with artists, one of whom – Rémy Zaugg – is almost a fifth partner. One of the first artists they worked with was Joseph Beuys in 1978; he opened their eyes beyond the supposed reality or objectivity of materials to the myriad associative meanings materials assume through memory and use. The late pop artist Andy Warhol is another figure they admire for the way he could make something new from everyday images, from well-known forms and materials. For the catalogue to accompany their exhibition design for the Swiss Pavilion at the fifth International Exhibition of Architecture at the Venice Biennale in 1991, Herzog & de Meuron asked fine-art photographers Margherita Krischanitz, Balthasar Burkhard, Hannah Villiger and Thomas Ruff to photograph some of their buildings. They simply find artists more innovative, more energetic, more personally involved, more willing to pursue the fantastic than architects are, and this helps Herzog & de Meuron to sustain their restless daring. The milieu from which their architecture emerges is speculative, cultural and intellectual. This can be seen in 'The Archaeology of the Mind' exhibition at the Canadian Centre for Architecture (2002). Curated by Philip Ursprung, it brazenly puts things that Herzog & de Meuron work with – bits of material and working models – alongside works of art. The result is akin to an archaeological investigation or the unfiltered collection of a natural history museum.

I use the term contemporary Swiss architecture with a certain liberty, as this book contains architects from the German-speaking areas only and includes one engineer. The work that has attained such regard in the last decade or so has come almost exclusively from Basel, Zurich and Graubünden. There is still very good work being produced in Ticino, though mostly from the same generation that brought it renown earlier.[3] French-speaking Switzerland, despite having its own ETH, has produced few postwar architects to rival those from Ticino or the

German-speaking areas.[4] Switzerland has a tradition of engineering excellence, encapsulated in the founding of ETH in Zurich in 1855 (the only federal institution of higher education until the creation in 1953 of its French-language counterpart in Lausanne, EPF). Its remit was to train engineers and technicians – and architects – to build modern Switzerland. Gottfried Semper was its first professor of design. Industrialization's need for efficient transport in a mountainous country like Switzerland meant bridges, tunnels and dams. The lineage of eminent bridge builders includes Robert Maillart, Othmar Ammann, Christian Menn and now Jürg Conzett.

Part of Switzerland's tradition of tolerance comes from its very artificiality as a country. It is a confederation of twenty-three cantons (of which three are divided into half cantons), where political power is highly devolved. Strong regional identities, including architectural, persist within small boundaries but its situation as a geographical crossroads has made Switzerland long subject to foreign influences and linked it to both northern and southern Europe. There are four official languages and English is widely understood. While predominantly Protestant, it has a sizeable Catholic population and both are state religions. It is disparate in every sense, its defining characteristic being that for centuries it has thrived on those differences.

The work in this book reflects that ultimate Swiss characteristic of pragmatic tolerance arising out of a confederation of disparate things. Even the two most obvious similarities leave rather a lot of room for difference: a relationship to minimal art's formal reduction, material precision and interest in Gestalt psychology; and the possibilities that present themselves when construction and enclosure diverge. The subsequent development of the skin shows a modernist sensibility employing the high-quality hand-crafting still available in the construction trades; things are rarely used straight out of the box. Yet it is the differences between architects that are more interesting than the similarities and these are what the individual chapters demonstrate. The most

marked changes to architecture in the last thirty years have resulted from the phenomenal growth and prominence of a developed-world culture industry. The sheer number of publications and rise in production values, the increasing visual sophistication of the public and increased mobility thanks to the EU and plummeting airfares have delivered the smaller, more homogeneous world that has long been forecast. Switzerland, typically, stands just outside this paradigm, taking it in, absorbing and adapting it, steadfastly building its own breed of extraordinary architecture.

Notes

[1] Kenneth Frampton's ill-tempered and oft-repeated outburst at overly artistic tendencies in Swiss architecture (*Daidalos*, Berlin, 1995) was misplaced. If there is one thing that characterizes the work, it is its embrace of building.
[2] Stanislaus van Moos. *Minimal Tradition: Max Bill and 'Simple' Architecture 1942–1996* (Baden: Lars Müller, 1996).
[3] Livio Vacchini in particular is producing startling work right now. Mario Botta has become world-famous and was instrumental in founding the Accademia di Architettura in 1996 to give the Italian-speaking population its own architecture school and indeed its own university.
[4] The reasons for this are the subject of debate, especially since Geneva led the way in the 1950s in large-scale housing. In the Suisse Romande it is such a sensitive issue that a recent architectural guide is actually entitled *La Romandie Existe*.

Bearth + Deplazes

Chairlift Station, Arosa,
Graubünden
[pp. 14–15] Base station
of the chairlift slipped
under the thin surface of
the landscape.

[opposite] The irregular
form, like a topographic
map, filled in with translucent sheets.

The work of Valentin Bearth and Andrea Deplazes shows little stylistic coherence, and they gladly admit to not being anchored to any single theoretical position. They do, however, have two consistent interests: context and construction. The possibilities and constraints inherent in building and place are fully considered in two of their projects in the resort town of Arosa, near Chur. The first project is for a chairlift station, an unusual commission for architects and a difficult one, not only because of exacting technical requirements but also because of the challenge of placing any kind of building in such a sublime landscape. There are two obvious and antithetical strategies. One is defensive, minimizing any intervention as if to acknowledge that architecture itself in such a dramatic landscape is undesirable. A second strategy is monumental, perhaps a conquering and fetishized piece of engineering. Typically, Bearth + Deplazes find a synthesis between the topographic and the technical.

Tourist infrastructure litters the landscape of Graubünden. Not only do such buildings have contemporary service requirements, but they are also often larger than traditional mountain buildings. For the base station of the chairlift the architects carve into the mountain and then pull the thin surface of the rocky landscape over it. They thus instigate a dialogue between built and natural forms and their representation. From up the hill all one sees are the openings for the chairs. The building has no proper mass and its silhouette is literally defined by the topography. On the downhill side, by contrast, skiers enter a glaring neon-orange tunnel, whose blatant artificiality and exposed structure contradict the naturalistic setting and make clear the artifice necessary to build in the landscape. But it also concedes the sheer fun of skiing; the palette is based on that of sports clothing and accessories. The structure is simple and pragmatic – a steel skeleton with vertically hung polycarbonate sheets that fill in this gentle rift in the earth's crust. They look brittle and crystalline in the changing light of day, like ice, even, and in the evening glow colourfully from inside. At the top station, at the 2,500-metre summit, there is even less pretence at being naturalistic. It is unabashedly bold and expressive, literally leaning out to scoop you up. It is also archetypal, referring to a roof or a tent. The inner space is painted the shrill orange colour of the lower station to make the connection with the beginning of the journey. The middle station is lime green.

While a chairlift is not quite a folly, it does fit into landscape traditions. Bearth + Deplazes's proposed conversion of the ice-rink site near the lake in Arosa into a small conference centre raises more traditional urban issues but the basic approach is similarly economical in concept. Like most such resorts in the Alps, Arosa is looking for ways to bring in visitors off-season but also to give non-skiers in winter something to do. Tantalizingly, the rink is

Chairlift Station, Arosa, Graubünden
[below] The brittle-looking polycarbonate skin refers to the snowy surroundings. Plan [opposite, top left] and section [opposite, top right] of the top station of the chairlift.
[opposite, below] The open entrance of the base station with its shrill interior.

situated at the town's entrance, where it may act as a landmark. Furthermore, the existing structure is exuberant, consisting of pairs of steel stanchions at the ends with suspension cables and a large truss in the centre from which the roof is suspended. Thus the architects' approach is to heighten the sculptural character of what is already there while enhancing the site's urban potential. They preserve the central rink but fill the perimeter of the site with shops, a restaurant, a multi-purpose hall, conference rooms and a foyer. Bringing the whole together is a skin of ruby-red glass that wraps around the perimeter and is pragmatically pierced wherever the architects need to create entrances to the different programmes. While old and new thus meld, their separate characters are still identifiable. The luminous, sensuous colour and effects of the glass play off the technophilic structure of the now off-centre roof.

These two themes of adapting to the immediate context and experimenting with cutting-edge construction technology have been consistent since Bearth and Deplazes founded the practice in 1988. They belong to the tradition of architecture as Baukunst, the art of building. Indeed, Deplazes is professor of architecture and construction at ETH Zurich. The partners made a name for themselves in the mid-1990s by exploring the rapid evolution of timber construction, both in practice and in theory, with a number of built houses and articles. While other Swiss

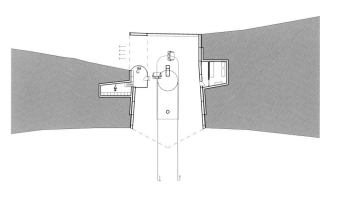

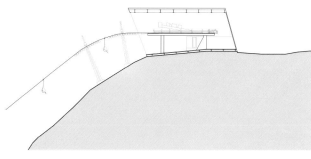

architects also looked at the way in which new methods of timber engineering in the 1990s challenged our preconceptions of its tectonics, Bearth and Deplazes became increasingly interested in advances in prefabrication. In particular, they considered how the move from the classic frame structure to something much freer, thanks to a rediscovery of modular prefabrication, meant that wood systems could compete directly with masonry and concrete structures.

Their research into timber construction has evolved into a general shift away from building in layers, with its preoccupation with skin, to building with mass and roughness. In an age still obsessed with surface and image, this is a radical, if inevitable step. The tall, single-family House Meuli, for example, is a massive construction of Stampfbeton, a primitive concrete system without reinforcement. The walls must therefore be thick, 50 cm, and are poured in a single layer into cheap formwork. For insulation the concrete is mixed with granulated glass (Miropor), making it relatively porous. The house is decidedly anti-high-tech. It is very tactile, rough, even, and one is always aware of the simple construction. The interior, however, is a more sophisticated play between mass and surface. Every wall and ceiling is covered with whitewash and the concrete floors are painted white. The interior space thus becomes continuous, a membrane, the material more plastic than massive. It seems to lose

House Meuli, Fläsch,
Graubünden
[pp.20–21] House seen
from the vineyard side
[left] and from the
street [right].

House Meuli, Fläsch,
Graubünden
[below] Corner of the
house, showing the
thickness of the walls.
Ground-floor plan
[opposite,top left] and

first-floor plan [opposite,
top right].
[opposite, below] The
house seen from the
village with the grape
vines climbing up the hill
in the background.

some of its texture, although, since whitewash is translucent, the qualities of the material do come through.

The simple building technology of the house is in keeping with the character of utilitarian buildings in wine-making villages like this. Switzerland is, of course, mountainous but almost all cantons produce wine, and vineyards are squeezed into every patch of suitable land. In the tradition of using as little land as possible, the form of the house is simply extruded from the plot and the vines cross the street to come up to the house itself. The resulting irregular form is ingeniously planned and the top-floor space is calm and impressive. As in the old vintners' houses, the windows are placed not to enhance the façade but according to interior considerations. But this is a house for young executives and accordingly, unlike in the old houses, the long façade faces the vineyards.

The architects' dual interests in working critically with the site and using new forms of construction are further demonstrated in their Contemporary Art Gallery in Marktoberdorf near Munich. The choice of massive construction and attendant rough textures gives it the character of an atelier rather than the supposed neutrality of the standard white gallery. The brick walls are of massive cheap clinker without insulation, laid with fat mortar joints. The heating pipes run through the walls. The wooden floorboards are likewise heavy and simply sit on steel beams, uninsulated,

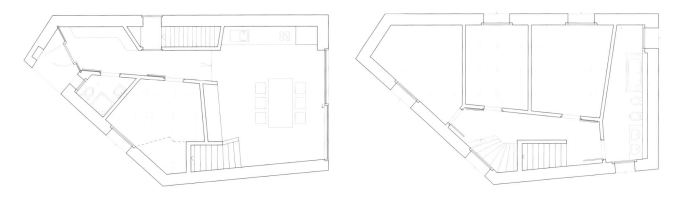

House Meuli, Fläsch, Graubünden
[left] Cross-section.
[below] House Meuli in relation to the village's traditional architecture and the landscape.

The top-floor study [opposite, left] and the stairs leading up to it [opposite, right].

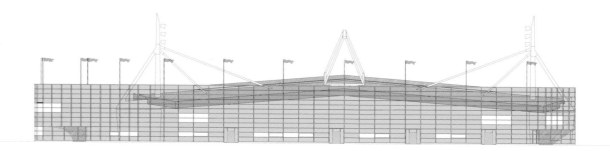

Ice-rink conversion, Arosa, Graubünden
[opposite, top] Elevation of the proposed conversion with the original structure sticking above the new skin.

[opposite, below] The bright-red skin.
[below] The structure's location on the corner lets it function as a gateway to the town.

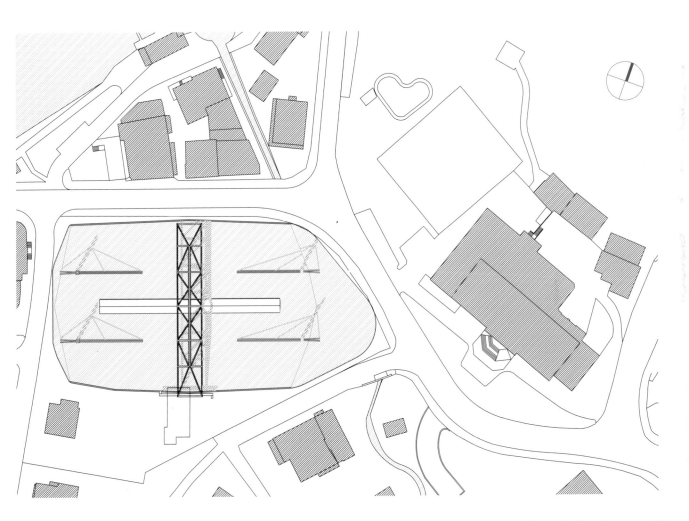

Contemporary Art Gallery,
Marktoberdorf, Germany
Street façade [opposite,
top] and entry façade
[opposite, below].
[below] Interior of
first floor.

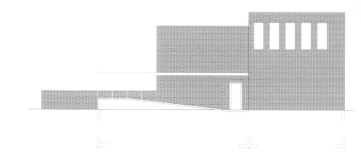

Contemporary Art Gallery,
Marktoberdorf, Germany
[opposite, top] Street
(west) elevation.
[opposite, below] Art on
display on the first floor.

[right] Ground-floor plan
with existing villa on
the right.
[below] The ground floor
with its triple-height space.

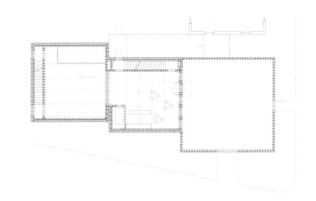

so that footsteps resonate through the floors below. The highly tectonic expression of the construction also challenges the bourgeois niceties and façade of the existing villa, although the programme of course accepts many of them. The gallery provides a sharp contrast between a highly haptic and acoustically lively experience and the experience of contemplating art, between the sturdiness of the building and the transience and perhaps fragility of the works displayed.

Although Bearth and Deplazes do not delineate separate roles in the office, their interests are neatly encapsulated in their biographies. Both graduated from ETH Zurich in the 1980s, but the five-year difference between them represents a key period at the school. Bearth completed his studies in 1983 with the then doyen of Swiss architecture, Dolf Schnebli, and afterwards worked for four years for Peter Zumthor when he was building small, refined timber buildings. Deplazes studied under Fabio Reinhardt and graduated in 1988. If Schnebli represented the epitome of a carefully constructed, highly crafted Swiss modernism, Reinhardt opened up the agenda to such hitherto taboo issues as historicism, memory and image, the quotidian and its poetic qualities. The partners have in common an education that encourages a quest for the quiet harmony and expressiveness of the site and programme within a modernist formal vocabulary, and a rigorous and inquisitive attitude towards construction.

Burkhalter Sumi Architekten

EMPA renovation,
Dübendorf, Zurich
Workshop entrances
[pp. 32–33] and front
entrances [below and
opposite, below].

Sections showing the
building after [opposite,
top left] and before
[opposite, top right]
the addition of the hall.

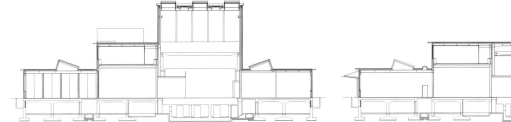

Swiss modernism's transformation into a canon in the 1960s carried with it the danger of ossification, of an architecture that was no more than a well-crafted, unspectacular refinement of a set of norms with little scope for innovation or risk. And indeed, much Swiss architecture is characterized by just such desiccated modernism, often overly detailed. A truer legacy, one within which Burkhalter Sumi Architekten are working, goes back further, to Le Corbusier's call for *recherche architecturale*. This kind of research rejects the conceptual or graphic deliberations that have traditionally come out of New York and London, the software fantasies of the technophiles and the current extravagant musings of the Dutch. It is firmly grounded in architecture and, importantly, in building. It follows a formal agenda and accepts certain tenets of modernism.

A good example of this approach is the series of buildings constructed between 1984 and 1995 in which Marianne Burkhalter and Christian Sumi methodically investigated the implications of building in timber. In a catalogue and exhibition marking the end of this period they relate their various influences and approaches. They had always been fascinated, like many architects, by the craft obvious in any timber vernacular, be it the scale, form and colour of grain silos and barns in North America, the plasticity of shingled churches of the Russian Orthodox faith or the materiality and directness of rural buildings in the Alps.

EMPA renovation,
Dübendorf, Zurich
[opposite] Entry to the renovated hall.
[below] The hall's folded,
solid and translucent ceiling.

They were also intrigued by a lesser-known practice in modern timber construction, which embraced prefabrication and industrialization in the building process. In Konrad Wachsmann's work they found the development of a universal standard connection but in Frank Lloyd Wright's Usonian Houses exactly the opposite – the standardization of the building's components and a sculptural power; in Jean Prouvé they found the concept of technology transfer, where the two-legged column was originally conceived in steel and is ambivalent between structure and shell; in Arne Jacobsen and Mies van der Rohe they found hybrid structures that allowed for large spans and, radically, the suppression of timber architecture's tradition of showing the story of its construction.

Over years of observations, contemplation and following their personal tastes, the architects accumulated a host of complicated and contradictory issues that they needed to work through and understand. Characteristically, they insisted on keeping the theoretical discourse as close as possible to building, as the eight wall sections at the back of the exhibition catalogue well demonstrate. Each represents a different timber construction technology that importantly leads to another architecture. With these little buildings the architects challenged such time-honoured precepts as the additive and didactic nature of timber architecture, showing that wood had become, in effect, a high-tech material.

Multi-Family Villas, Witikon, Zurich
[left] The villas on Zurich's gold coast.

[below] Ground-floor plan for House 8.

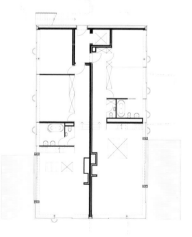

Multi-Family Villas, Witikon, Zurich
[right] One of the bright-red villas with varied openings providing different types of enclosure and views. [below] Ground-floor plan for House 6.

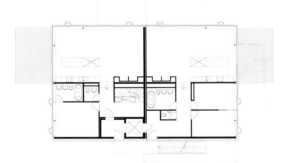

Multi-Family Villas,
Witikon, Zurich
[opposite] The villas sit
parallel or perpendicular
to the slope of the hill.
[below] An exterior
staircase.

Such rigour alone would separate their work from most, but what makes it especially distinctive is that it is lively and sensuous too. The architects' best-known building from this period is a prototype for standardized forestry stations. They broke the programme down into three components – administration, garage and open hall – which they could arrange according to different site conditions. The open hall's five-metre-span roof expresses almost nothing of its construction or statics, being dematerialized to a red plane sitting on tree trunks stripped of their bark. The other two components are wrapped in a timber skin that is sometimes used to bring elements together but at other times to separate them. This is achieved through the simple means of colour, finish and the direction in which the boards are laid. The forestry stations are simultaneously rigorous and playful, abstract and figurative.

Their quest to understand timber construction involved Burkhalter and Sumi in confronting such fundamental architectural issues as form and tectonics. That modern construction is in layers means that skin, structure and space are potentially separate from one another. But how then to achieve a building that is not simply fragmented? Their response was to look to form and our perception of it, a view underpinned by their research into Gestalt psychology and their theory of tectonics. In various articles and debates they have argued that the

Multi-Family Villas,
Witikon, Zurich
[below and opposite] The
timber skin and colour

unify the form and help
differentiate types
of openings.

industrialization of the construction industry and the increasing use of composites have resulted in a loss of meaning in materials. For example, it can be argued that there is no such thing as wood, only wood products. From that premise one could then proceed in various ways: instil meaning into the materials; refuse to use them; adopt a completely artistic or aesthetic approach; or, perversely, eradicate any vestigial meaning or nature as far as possible. They chose this last course and in projects such as the Business School in Laufenberg use materials in such a way as to confuse the inside and the outside, the large and the small, the natural and the artificial. But if materials have no inherent meanings, the challenge is to find the right material. Burkhalter and Sumi looked to use materials for their effect, be it perceptual or formal. In the Hotel Zürichberg, for example, wood cladding is used horizontally as a skin to reinforce the squat form of the oval; applied colour is used inside to heighten the sense of a circular and an elliptical space spiralling around each other.

Underpinning Burkhalter Sumi Architekten's constructional, material and formal investigations has been their typological work of the 1970s, best seen in their housing projects. Typology must be understood here not as a catalogue of solutions but as a discipline within which to work creatively. It is a way of dealing with form without being formalist. This is illustrated in their South Gallery

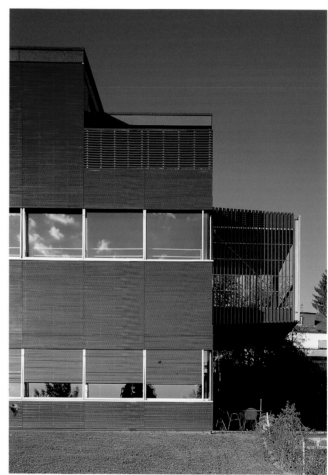

House in Laufenberg (1996), a seamless conjunction of various types. For instance, they invert the classical modernist plan by putting the circulation on the south side. But they conform to Alpine types, where the big sheltered outdoor space facing south is used for socializing and drying crops, by placing a broad gallery here. Furthermore, they introduce the currently unpopular typology of deck-access housing to this south side but ingeniously cut holes in it and create entrance boxes so as to preserve privacy.

Of course housing raises larger issues of people's changing lifestyles and the way in which architects respond to these changes – for example, the dissolution of the nuclear family and an increase in home working – and about where people live, for much housing is now neither urban nor suburban. In the project on Zurich's 'gold coast' in Witikon, included in this chapter, we see Burkhalter and Sumi working on a new housing type, the multi-family villa, by developing modernist Swiss and Italian upper-class urban flats of the 1930s. The three buildings have different floor plans according to their setting and volume. Both the materials and the colours are contextual and the general massing keeps them within the tradition of villas in a park. But the way these things are handled sets them apart and again Burkhalter and Sumi work with types. The windows and balconies, for instance, are based on the framed view and the picture view, the

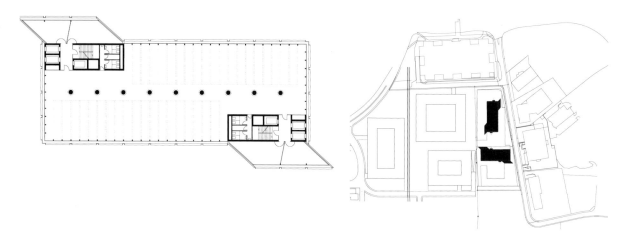

latter being conceived like the modernist strip window. The framed view derives from a much older tradition, where the viewer is always looking through an intermediate zone to the outside. This type is executed in the form of large terraces and huge viewing boxes, a solid/void game. The boxes, seemingly slung on to the exterior, function almost like viewing machines or oculi, the lattices on the sides providing literally a filter. The loggias are both objects and spaces or exterior rooms. The landscaping (by Günther Vogt) similarly starts from what already exists and develops something new from it. It provides the privacy and sense of ownership owners of such expensive flats would expect, while still referring to the area's allotments.

This tireless self-questioning to which the architects submit themselves is hard work but they consider it fundamental: 'Like Roland Barthes's Argonauts who continually renew their spaceship during flight, without "intermediate landing or interruption", architects must also continually reconstruct the edifice of their theoretical knowledge.' But it is important to note that this is relieved by a lightness of touch that prevents their work from being didactic. This synthesis between the conceptual and sensual, typology and invention, art and technology is mirrored in the architects' biographies (though not in their working method). The contemplative Sumi had a classical Swiss architect's education. He studied at ETH during the period when modernism was presented as a set of rules, and stayed on as a research assistant, working on the schemes of Le Corbusier. But outside ETH the avant-garde was challenging just this institutionalization and canonization of modernism by the introduction of play or even mischief. It was in this latter milieu that Burkhalter learned architecture, having trained as a draughtsman before working with Superstudio in Florence, attending classes at Princeton University and working with Studio Works in New York and Los Angeles.

Burkhalter Sumi Architekten's work in this chapter shows a development of the previously discussed issues but also the prominence of new ones, particularly of their interest in the period of the Smithsons and architecture's social meaning. The opportunity to renovate a materials testing lab (EMPA), which is a good example of 1960s architecture, with its frame, infill and steel windows, has been particularly inspiring for them. These postwar buildings are part of a living tradition, but their environmental and material performance are now well out of date. The architects treat the complex with respect but not archaeologically. Indeed, many of the materials originally used are no longer available or suitable. The primary structure can be preserved while the fabric and interiors are transformed. The complex of buildings can be given new functions, densified and added to rather than preserved. The architects then treat the buildings

Office Centre, Opfikon, Zurich

[opposite, left] Floor plan with meeting rooms breaking out at the corners.

[opposite, right] Site plan of the two towers.
[below] Rendering of a tower.

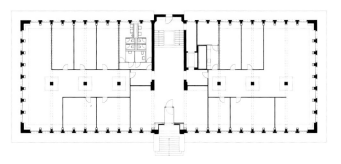

Sulzer Building renovation, Winterthur
[opposite, top] The stiff monumentality of the existing entrance.
[opposite, below] The original building.
[left] The renovated ground-floor plan.
[below] The entry protrudes into the foyer.

Sulzer Building renovation, Winterthur
[right] Cross-section with rooftop addition.
[below] Interior of entrance with light installations by Mayo Bucher.

[opposite] Interior with exposed column and beam.

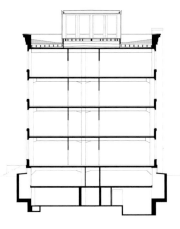

as found and new elements as new. A colour palette from the 1950s is used to bring things together. The scheme is a subtle balance between old and new, respect and renewal.

The renovation of a monumental, 1930s neoclassical office building for a large industrial company likewise confronted the architects with the 'as-found'. Unconventionally, they pushed the services to the perimeter, thus opening up the centre. They then emphasized the long, central axis with a tectonic play among beams, pillars and consoles, which is given a site-specific context by the use of integrated, industrial-like lighting. Likewise, with the penthouse addition, the architectural strategy is not to contrast with what exists but to heighten its character. This pavilion thus mimics the heaviness and the unrelenting rhythm of the existing building although built of timber, not concrete. The penthouse accepts the building's neoclassical lineage, sitting within a garden to which one cannot gain access; it is something to view, not physically occupy.

Burkhalter and Sumi argue that the seemingly irreconcilable aspects of the various requirements that condition the design of a building cannot be eliminated but only resolved. As they describe their own approach, they 'tread the narrow path between traditional design concerns such as programme, space, representation, tectonics

Sulzer Building renovation, Winterthur
[below and opposite, top] The top-floor addition with a rooftop terrace and garden.
[opposite, below] The sculptural play of the renovation.

and the radical questioning of fundamental precepts with a curiosity and openness with regard to new approaches'. This approach necessarily rejects stylistic consistency and means that while the work from the office is recognizable, it also shows remarkable development. The Office Centre, Opfikon, while pushing the office into a larger scale of work and a commercial, speculative development, still manages to question many of the basic tenets of such buildings. Radically, the traditional service core, with its lifts, cold and warm water, sprinkler pipes and ducting, is situated on the exterior. But, rather than allow this to be visible, the architects conceal it in the two-layered curtain wall, necessary for local acoustical reasons. The centre is now free spatially and the building can be perceived from the inside in its entirety. The corners are not lost, however, but are extended beyond the perimeter to form perfect meeting rooms as well as to give the building a sculptural presence with new possibilities for the façade.

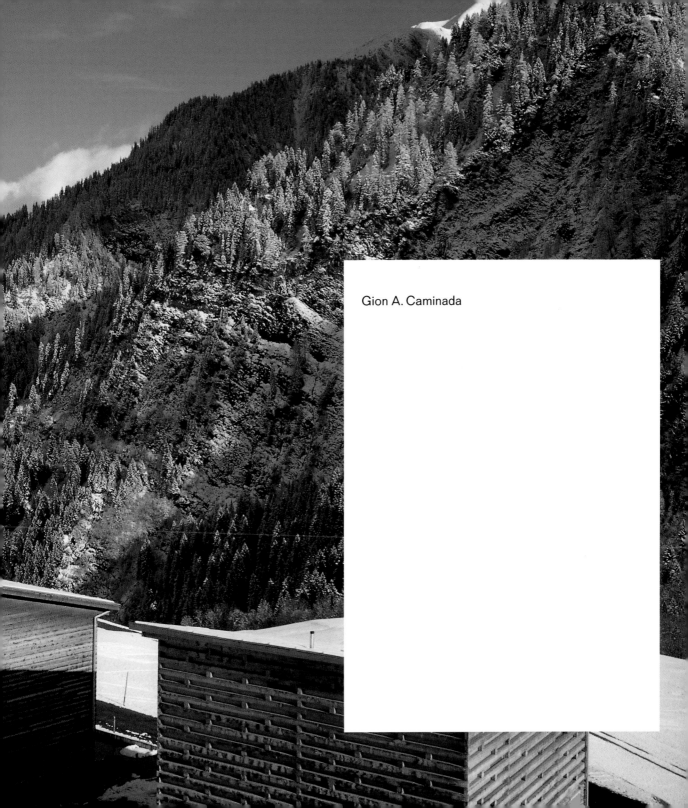

Gion A. Caminada

Switzerland presents two faces to the world that seem mutually exclusive. One image is of an ordered, wealthy and urbanized country that makes money from finance, high-end tourism, quality chocolates and precision watches. The other image is of an equally tidy but bucolic landscape of farmers, cows and cheese. Remarkably, both images are correct. The survival of the latter in a difficult mountain environment and in the face of encroaching urban development has been much aided by the country's policy of armed neutrality, which regards food production as an issue of domestic security. Moreover, it is only in the last two generations that modernization has seriously impacted on the country and the Swiss themselves retain a sentimental attachment to their mountains, villages and traditional ways of life. This larger context is relevant to the work of Gion A. Caminada, one of 280 inhabitants of Vrin, the village at the far end of the high, Romansch-speaking valley of Lumnezia.

Switzerland is not immune to the European-wide trends in agriculture towards mechanization and amalgamation that necessitate larger farms and buildings, but Vrin decided that it would resist abandoning its centuries-old way of life and transforming itself into a tourist centre or weekend retreat. It wanted to remain a working village, and this meant keeping the farmer there. The Pro Vrin foundation was established in 1979 to preserve its way of life and

<u>Stalls and Abattoir, Vrin, Graubünden</u>
[pp. 54–55 and opposite, top] The stalls and abattoir on the edge of the village.

[opposite, below and below] The stone base of the abattoir.
[right] Ground-floor plans with the smaller abattoir on the left.

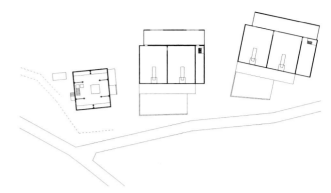

Totenstube, Vrin,
Graubünden
[below] The Totenstube
with the village church in
the background.

[opposite] The entrance for
the casket on the right and
for mourners on the left.

cultural landscape. A three-part strategy comprised the extension and modernization of existing buildings; construction on the edge of the village; and an area near the village for stalls. Caminada, whose roots go back generations in the valley and whose office is in one of its four outlying settlements, acts as planner and architect.

Centuries of living in a harsh alpine climate that is still remote in winter have strongly influenced the village's character, development and architecture. The fundamental starting point in developing the village was respect for its additive nature, existing typology and materials. At the same time, the residents have modern needs and expectations, so a nostalgic recreation of historic types would be inappropriate. The town hall, for example, is converted from an old farmhouse, which typically has residence, cowshed and vegetable garden forming a small courtyard. Caminada respects this typology but makes the old and the new halves visible. He replaces the animal stalls with offices. The community hall would be too large there, and is instead placed next to the school at the edge of the village. Along with the church it dominates the village, but the distinction between sacred and profane is maintained. The elegant truss system in the hall is cleverly engineered so that it could be built by local tradesmen with local timber. The ties are built up of five laths 24 mm thick nailed together only at the centre and fanning out towards the edge of the room where they

Totenstube, Vrin,
Graubünden
[below] Ground-floor plan.
[top] Upper- or church-
level plan.

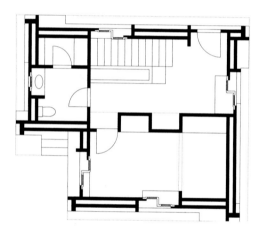

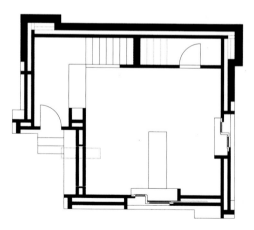

meet timber columns. Caminada has also built a single-family house, an addition to a woodworking shop and a telephone booth.

To date Caminada has mostly employed solid timber construction, known in Swiss-German as *Strickbau* ('knit-building'), a term that refers to the interlocking corners of such work. It is a type of construction in which structure equals surface. Traditionally of round logs, it now consists of two layers of milled timber with insulation in between. The interior wood lining envelops you in its warmth. The other tradition is the stone base, which for practical reasons is often replaced by concrete.

The needs of such remote villages may seem uncommon to the visitor, and afford the architect some unusual briefs and opportunities. When someone in the village died the body was traditionally laid out in his or her sitting room until the funeral in the church, the centre of village life. But attitudes to death have changed and the villagers decided that they wanted an intermediate place for the deceased between home and church. The term 'village mortuary' conveys none of the poetry of the Swiss-German word *Totenstube*, nor the domestic connotations of its design as a resting place for the dead that is a space for the living as well (*Stube* in dialect is the living room or kitchen). Public buildings in small villages must serve many functions. This is not therefore just a house

<u>Totenstube, Vrin,
Graubünden</u>
[below left] Windows
pushed outwards and
inwards and the central
pillar afford discretion and
a variety of experiences.
[below right] The view
from below the village.

Gion A. Caminada   61

for the dead. With poetic symbolism, the architect has adopted the typology of the house, which is earthbound and quotidian, but sited it just outside the churchyard – the body's final destination – where the church next door holds out the promise of heaven. The top floor is at graveyard level and contains a kind of waiting room, toilets and a small kitchen. Downstairs, at village level, is a large room with two exterior doors, one for the coffin and one for mourners. The windows are set both towards the inside and towards the exterior in pairs, with a hefty post in the centre that affords discretion. While the church is rendered in white plaster, the Totenstube and almost all other buildings in the village are made of massive timber, though in this case whitewashed. The interior surface is shellacked. The base is not the traditional stone but poured concrete, partly because of the building's stepped form.

As part of the project's aim is to sustain the community, virtually all the materials and the craftsmen Caminada uses are from the valley. Wealth is thus created and benefits the local people directly. To build here, however, requires much discussion and patience. It can take years before agreement is reached. But the labour-intensive construction process based on consensus and the developed typologies is evidence of the social value of architecture. Although the construction methods are traditional, the styles and forms acknowledge contemporary

Totenstube, Vrin, Graubünden
[opposite] The varnished and golden wood interiors of the upper or church level.

[below] The ground floor with the space for the casket on the right.

Single-family house,
Vignon, Graubünden
Single-family house based
on a rural typology with the
traditional crossing of
walls in *Strickbau*.

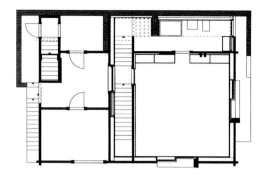

methods and needs. Windows were traditionally small to help keep the inside warm, for example, but nowadays people demand more light and it is possible to provide larger windows with better insulation. Caminada understands that for city people nature is beautiful and big windows allow them to view it, whereas those who work in the mountains know that nature is also harsh, even cruel, and prefer intimacy and warmth. Rooms have thus tended to be cosy and inward-looking.

That architecture is a fundamental and even necessary act can sometimes be difficult to remember when one reads the latest professional literature and hears new paradigms discussed. And Caminada's architecture does seem more immediate than most. He is surely one of only a handful of contemporary architects to design a noteworthy set of stables and an abattoir (used once a week on a Thursday), an economically vital set of buildings for the village. The client was the local cooperative, which understood the importance of higher returns from processing and marketing their meats, sausages and cheeses themselves. The three buildings are sited in an irregular chain down the hill from the church, respecting the latter's pre-eminence but remaining convenient to animal herders. The building nearest the village, with an almost square plan and rubble stone exterior base, has a ground floor containing the abattoir and butchery area and an attic traditionally used for curing. The stalls are longer, based

Single-family house, Vignon, Graubünden
Ground-floor [opposite, top left] and first-floor [opposite, top right] plans show the division of the house by the staircase. [opposite, below and below] The combination of traditional building techniques and a modern vocabulary.

Hotel Alpina, Vals,
Graubünden
[below and opposite]
The renovated façade on the main square contrasts
with the language of
the traditional village
architecture.

on traditional barns but with modern touches. For instance, the slatted hayloft also admits machinery, and there are ribbon windows above the stall doors.

Caminada has taken on other commissions outside the village but retains his fundamental principles. In the case of the single-family house in Vignon in the same valley, the client had built before but this time was looking for somewhere to retire and had singled out this particular valley. He hired Caminada because he wanted a house that would not compromise the values and way of life in the valley that he so admired. The architect based the house on a traditional scheme, which has a heated part for human habitation and an unheated part for livestock and agricultural storage. He then developed this type into a house suitable for modern living, with the stairwell joining the two halves horizontally as well as vertically. The main room is based on the traditional farmhouse *Stube*, or living room or kitchen. It is not grand but rather warm and cosy, although more lavishly appointed than the rest of the house, with oak floor, walls and ceiling. (The rest of the house is made of fir and larch to save on cost.) For this room Caminada designed a bronze wood oven with a visible flame. The bathrooms are covered in a local granite from Vals. The uninsulated half faces south and west to the view and is heated passively. Even in the winter one can sit on the terrace on a sunny day.

Hotel Alpina, Vals,
Graubünden
[opposite and below]
The reduced vocabulary
of the entrance.

Hotel Alpina, Vals,
Graubünden
[opposite, top] First-floor
plan with restaurant and
the three renovated
bedrooms.

[opposite, below] One
of the rooms renovated
by Caminada, with a
variation on the traditional
window seat.

In Vals Caminada was faced with a more typical commission from private clients. The town, which lies in a parallel valley to Vrin, is the source for a well-known mineral water and has been a resort since the 1950s. The number of visitors has soared, however, with the completion of Peter Zumthor's thermal baths in 1997. The third-generation owners of the Hotel Alpina thought it time to renovate and hired Caminada. They wanted to rationalize the space inside and do something with the terrace, which could be used for only about three weeks in the year. But they were also aware of the hotel's prominent situation on the village square and near the church. Caminada removed the terrace and created a façade that better conformed with the space of the square. The material is not massive timber, although there are such buildings on the square, but the grey render matches that of the other hotels and restaurants near by and has a sparkle to it to catch the southern light. The windows are huge and wooden. On the interior a generous reception hall with stone floors, oak panelling and a massive vertical structure is created in a modern vernacular. The original wood-panelled restaurant on the ground floor has been retained and sits comfortably among the new features. On the first floor is another restaurant, also modern, but warm and presenting a happy balance between formal and informal. The architect has designed three new bedrooms.

Caminada himself acknowledges how strange and romantic his practice must look seen from the outside. In its context of Vrin, however, it seems perfectly plausible and admirable in its integrity and solidity. Caminada is currently a visiting professor at ETH Zurich and is heading a studio that is looking at mountain villages that no longer function effectively to see if architecture can restore them. The architecture applied in this context is not awe-inspiring or attention-seeking but the buildings feel as if they belong in their surroundings as well as in our time. They are refreshingly immediate.

Jürg Conzett

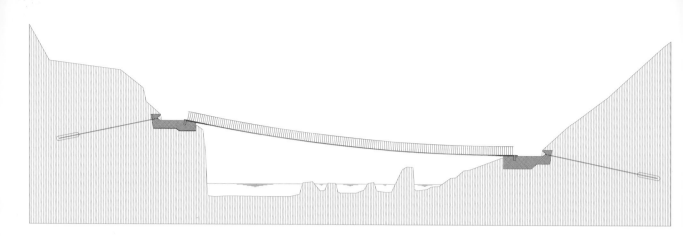

Before the architect became a professional in the modern sense in the eighteenth century, the distinction between the function of an architect and that of an engineer was often slight. As the two roles became more clearly delineated, their domains and cultures became more distinct, if not sometimes antagonistic. The consequence can still be seen in architecture's periodic swings between artistic and technological pretensions. The danger in the rationalization of engineering was that it could become a simple problem-solving service based on a scientific model.

The engineer Jürg Conzett, of architectural practice Conzett Bronzini Gartmann, is fascinated by the intellectual development of the Enlightenment that produced engineering schools, but is equally taken with the less rational engineering of other eras, such as the Baroque. If at that time one wasn't sure whether the arch on a bridge would suffice to support it, for instance, one might add a half-timbered structure just to be sure. Such superimpositions, the results of deduction, intuition and experience, characterize his own work. He likes projects that are interesting on many levels and cites the Albula railway of the early twentieth century, when old techniques were rediscovered and renewed and the best designers employed, because the relationship of the railway to the landscape, the layout of the tracks and the choice of materials were acknowledged to be important. Attaching value to inventiveness, as Conzett does, is not

Surasuns Footbridge,
Viamala, Graubünden
[pp. 74–75] The footbridge
draped across the river.
[opposite, top] Section
through the river banks.

[opposite, below and
below] Bridge leading out
of the woods and across
the river, mediating the
difference in height
between the two banks.

Surasuns Footbridge,
Viamala, Graubünden
[opposite] View from
underneath showing
stone, steel ribbons
and balustrade.

[below] The massive
foundations and the thin
bridge itself.

Surasuns Footbridge, Viamala, Graubünden
[left] Steel, stone and concrete at the bridge's edge.

[below] A delicate insertion in a sublime landscape.

the same as embracing expressiveness, adopting a signature style or pursuing a personal formal vocabulary. He accepts that being an engineer means eschewing extravagance: 'I think that engineering as a service to society is a beautiful idea. And with that idea one accepts a certain anonymity. There are many bridges whose designer no one knows and yet which are of high quality.' He is proud that the principles behind his efficient but otherwise unspectacular motorway bridges near Sufers have been copied by other engineers. But the designers in his practice first sketch out all possible solutions to generate yet more solutions and lay out for consideration the benefits in each. This is a way of resisting what Conzett calls a monoculture, where for purely economic reasons the fewest possible solutions are proffered.

Architects bemoan the shortage of creative engineers, and in a small country like Switzerland someone of his talent is of course much sought after. He has collaborated with every architect in this book. Conzett tries to work with architects who are interested in fundamental questions. He is one of those rare engineers who can truly collaborate with architects, but he expects a good architect to have already designed a sensible structure. He worked for Peter Zumthor for six years before setting up his own office and teaches engineers and architects at the interdisciplinary department of building at the HTW (Hochschule für Technik und Wirtschaft) in Chur.

Conzett likes a challenge. At the Swiss Timber Engineering School in Biel, he and the architects Marcel Meili and Markus Peter created an innovative timber building that follows many of the principles of concrete construction. He also needed to find a creative solution to the problem of the poor bearing capacity of the soil: the concrete slab was successively pre-tensioned as additional floors were added. For an office building in Chur Conzett and the architects Jüngling & Hagmann devised a perhaps unique structural system in the façade, with tension cables and prefabricated elements that allow a column-free interior. He took active part in the debates on the use of materials in the 1990s. His stance had nothing to do with the ethical implications of the so-called correct use of a material but with its actual qualities, as can be seen in his bridges featured in this chapter. He is currently trying to develop a true frame structure for large buildings from the principles of timber construction. A system of slabs and columns, for instance, does not allow floors to hang freely.

The clearest expression of Conzett's method and regard for practical, technical and cultural issues can be seen in his bridge designs. The outdoor Ecomuseum encompasses the Viamala, the longest gorge and the most direct route through the Alps from Lake Constance to Milan. It has been a main north–south passage since at least Roman times but has also been highly dangerous. Travellers were in danger from falling rocks as well as narrow and precarious paths, flash floods and blizzards. Nowadays roads and tunnels make the journey easier and remove the sense of danger. The proposed stair bridge in this chapter seeks to restore some of the sense of adventure to travelling through the gorge. It replaces the first Traversina Footbridge, which was about 70 metres away and was smashed by falling rocks three years after it was finished. Many of the same issues that had to be addressed then still apply: a remote site, a tight budget and a short construction period. The difficulty of access meant that the first bridge had to be transported to the site by helicopter and so had to be light. This was one reason to choose timber, but the other was that the region has a tradition of timber architecture, which Conzett thought was important. The solution for the 47-metre span was a lattice of triangles that fanned out over the centre of the gorge; panelled side rails above stiffened it, protected the lattice from the elements and acted as handrails. These sub- and superstructures were connected by vertical struts. 'It was,' says Conzett, 'a balancing act between weight and stability.'

The Surasuns Footbridge was likewise commissioned as part of the Ecomuseum and the design driven by similarly complex considerations. It was important that this bridge in the southern part of the trail be made of stone rather than timber as a reflection of the material and cultural distinctions between the northern and southern sides of the

Pedestrian Bridge, Bruges, Belgium
[opposite] The finishing piece in the cycle and pedestrian path.

[below] The massive pillars that support the rotating tubes.

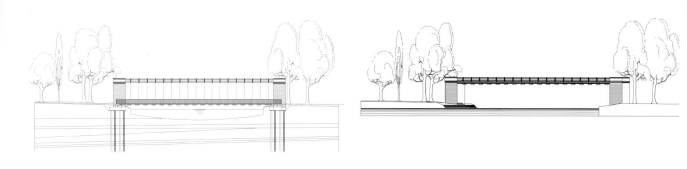

Pedestrian Bridge, Bruges, Belgium
Sections with the bridge lowered [opposite, left] and raised [opposite, right].

[opposite, below and below] The bridge crosses the Coupure Canal and completes an urban landscape.

Alps. The stone underfoot would also echo the flagstone paths along the way. The placement of the bridge in this steep gorge had to take account of access for walkers and could not be at the river's narrowest point. At the site chosen, the span across is 40 metres and there is a 4-metre difference in height between the banks.

The obvious apparent contradiction between using granite (locally quarried) and building a lightweight structure is one of the joys of the design. Conzett thought that a thin, pre-stressed stone covering would act in much the same way as a large monolithic slab and proposed a stress-ribbon system, which behaves similarly to a suspension bridge. The construction was tested using a 1:20 scale model to confirm the accuracy of the calculations. The abutments were cast in place and anchored into the banks but the rest of the construction is dry. The steel ribbons underneath were pre-tensioned, the granite slabs set out from the lower end, loosely bolted in place by means of the balustrade supports, and steel blocks inserted at either end to compress the slabs against each other and form an inverse arch. (In the abutments one can see where the temporary hydraulic jack was situated.) The nuts holding the slabs were then tightened and the handrail welded on to the supports. The greatest unknown was the oscillation, but the bridge has turned out to be remarkably stable, yet lively enough to give the user the feeling that its form suggests.

Footbridge, Viamala,
Graubünden
Plan [top] and section
[below] of the lightweight
timber footbridge.

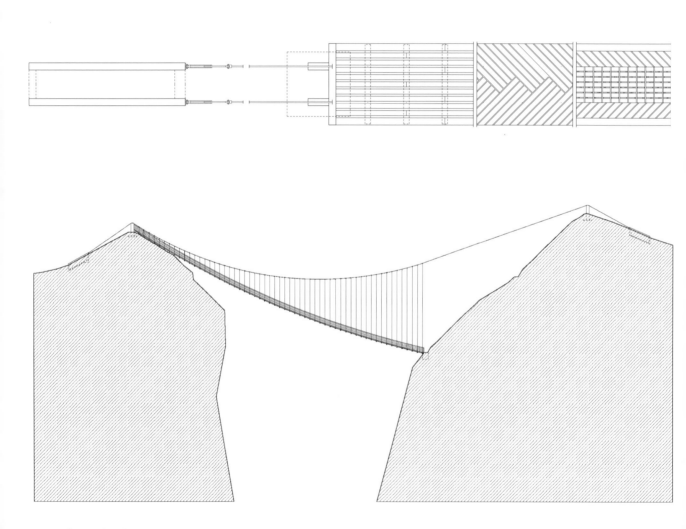

A perfect instance of Conzett's talents as architectural engineer can be seen in his pedestrian bridge in Bruges, a delightful piece of urban design (done in collaboration with Professor Jürg Meier). This was the missing link in the pedestrian and cycle path on the ramparts surrounding Bruges's city centre that had been a source of irritation for years. Thanks to this new bridge over the Coupure Canal, one no longer has to walk or cycle all the way round. The challenge was to make the bridge accessible to walkers and cyclists without too much of a slope while still allowing boats to pass underneath it. A traditional drawbridge would have required space on either side of the canal, but here there is an avenue of trees on one side, which would have had to be cut down, and the walls of a courtyard on the other. The solution is a kind of highly inventive lift-bridge. Conzett needed to take into consideration three levels: the water, the banks and the treetops. Two steel tubes, almost like tree trunks, are fixed over the canal's span of 36.5 metres at the height of the tree-tops. The tubes rotate to wind the suspension cables around them, thereby lifting the platform. But, to keep the tubes within scale they are pre-stressed on both sides of the piers, with the different direction of their forces. The posts are built of sandstone, again pre-stressed.

Even in Switzerland there is pressure on architects and engineers to keep their fees down. The great danger is that the architect and the engineer can no longer afford to work together from the beginning of a project. Worse still is the tendency to agree a fee before one really has the opportunity to know what the problem is. Blindly accepting the requirements of the contractor is not always in the best interests of the client; equally, blindly accepting what the client thinks he wants is an abdication of professional responsibility and often bad for the quality of design. As a professional Conzett has ideas that interest him and that he would like to pursue and develop, such as pre-tensioning, a technique most often used with concrete, but which he has increasingly used with timber. He is looking for ways to resist 'dumbing down', and recently organized a competition for an engineering project, in which the winner was awarded the contract.

Conzett deplores a culture that prizes building quickly and cheaply over all other considerations, but this does not mean that he can only work on special projects. 'Sometimes the obvious, inexpensive solution is also what is required architecturally and it takes sensitivity to recognize this. At other times, a more singular solution is needed to achieve architectural quality, which is also the engineer's responsibility.'

Diener & Diener

The development of the European city in terms of planning, architecture and social structure has been an urgent and contentious topic since industrialization. The myriad proposals and positions have ranged from utopian new worlds to the nostalgic reconstruction of old ones, or even from benign to malign neglect. Whether the city is even an architectural issue is a question that goes in and out of fashion, though it is certainly thought to be one now. In West Berlin in the 1980s the IBA (International Building Exhibition Berlin) pursued a reconstruction of the city's nineteenth-century urban form of large blocks with courtyards. After the wall came down, the dominant position was that the language and materials of the historic architecture of turn-of-the-century Berlin should form the basis for a massive building programme. As the storm over Berlin started to subside a more open-minded approach to the city came out of the Netherlands. It accepts postwar ways and images of living, though it sometimes seems too readily seduced by a laissez-faire, American model of suburbia. Over the same period but with less fanfare, Diener & Diener have been assiduously working on the European city of today, developing a position and an architecture that avoid the fallacies of each of the above approaches.

Diener & Diener developed their position through building in Basel, a city that has been important since the Middle Ages but which, like most Swiss cities, developed its pre-dominant urban and architectural form during the rapid industrialization of the second half of the nineteenth century. While this fabric is still intact, the urban form has also evolved through the impact of styles from the twentieth century, especially from the 1920s and the 1950s. The city thus tends to be more heterogeneous and also subtler than many rebuilt European cities and building well in it requires both sensitivity and precision.

A characteristic example by Diener & Diener is their Administration Building (1993) at Picassoplatz in Basel. The square is not a traditional one, but is a classic postwar configuration. The irregularly shaped space allowed for traffic has many vistas through it and is defined by nineteenth-century perimeter blocks, office buildings from the 1950s and 1960s with strong frontages, and important public buildings that refer to the square but do not face it. The architects accept this complexity of conditions. The ground plan of the building acknowledges the street line of the blocks and the spaces the public buildings leave, and presents frontages to the square and other vistas. The design of the façade reinforces the building's heaviness and ties the various responses together, although it is obviously a skin. There is a characteristic ambiguity of the window as a traditional void in the wall or as a curtain. This exploration made the relationship between inner and outer, between the architecture of the traditional and the modern cities, ambiguous.

Java Island housing,
Amsterdam, the
Netherlands
[pp. 88–89] The two
housing blocks seen
from the port.

[below] The cantilevered
entry to the courtyard
block.

It is through such Basel projects of the early 1990s,
where the traditional urban fabric and a looser, contemporary situation exist simultaneously, that Diener & Diener's
principles for the European city developed. The architecture was driven by the site so precisely that it
could belong there and nowhere else. The formal characteristics of the work remain from this period: simple,
severe volumes, clear façades with recognizable windows, a play of solid and void, buildings that are hard
and have a sense of weight. But this apparent simplicity
has nothing to do with a moral ascendancy sometimes
attached to such characteristics, that of the permanent
over the ephemeral, or the closed instead of the open.
Rather, such a restricted formal vocabulary allows the
architect to concentrate on small differences in the site
and programme and yet hold the building together. It is
eminently pragmatic, yet the buildings look both familiar
and a bit strange. The fruits of this approach were col-
lected in the exhibition and publication, 'The House and
the City', of 1995. Roger Diener likes to refer to their
buildings as houses, with the emphasis on the space
they occupy in the city and their relationship to the other
spaces of the city.

The architects' most recent work considers how to
respond where traditional and contemporary, closed
and open, clearly structured and seemingly random,
abut. Much of the severe formal vocabulary remains but

Java Island housing,
Amsterdam, the
Netherlands
[right] Site plan of both
buildings on either side of
the proposed causeway.

The long block [below]
and the courtyard block
[opposite].

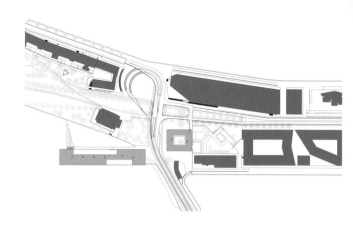

ABB Power Tower, Baden
[below] The protruding
corner of the new offices.
[opposite, clockwise from
top left] One of the courtyards; detail of the façade;
the precision and order
of the façade; the varied
character of the massing
and façades.

ABB Power Tower, Baden
[below] Shallow and deep balconies.
[opposite, below] Site plan showing the area's industrial character.

[opposite, top] The variation and coherence of the façades.

it has become even stricter and less mannered. A good example is their proposal for developing an industrial site of factories and offices on the northern edge of Baden into a mixed-use quarter. The complex is occupied by Asea Brown Boveri, a prominent Swiss–Swedish engineering and industrial conglomerate with its own architectural heritage. The idea is to respect its nature, and so the siting of the additional four buildings is driven by the logic of the industrial complex, namely, by programmatic and functional conditions and not by grand theories of urban planning. The additions are similarly autonomous, quiet, regularly shaped volumes arranged according to production requirements, with the public spaces accordingly workmanlike. The architectural language does not mimic industry for its practical effects but rather reflects its heritage back on itself.

Yet more complicated are the two sites for housing on either side of the causeway between KNSM and Java islands in the historical port of Amsterdam. The port is now obsolete and the Netherlands decided to resist its tendency towards suburbanization with dense planning. The original port buildings are big sheds that face out over the water and ignore any relationship to each other or to the inner side of the island across the way. The extensive new housing consists of almost every urban type, from row houses to courtyard types to super-blocks. Diener & Diener's commission was for the last

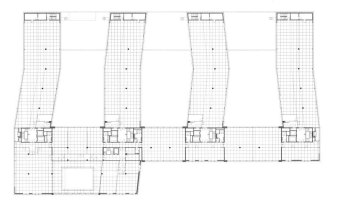

ABB Power Tower, Baden
[left] Typical floor plan.
[opposite and below] The
reduced vocabulary of
the interiors refers to the
area's industrial heritage
without mimicking it.

two buildings, and the site is between the block structure
in the eastern part and the courtyard structure in the west;
as well, there is a smattering of original port buildings,
including the Captain's house. Their two buildings sit on
either side of the pier at the middle point of the island
and mediate among these incompatible types by putting
everything into a precise state of unstable equilibrium.
This is a kind of radical contextualism and possibly the
only sensible strategy when there is no clear urban form
with which to work. The courtyard block sits alone in
the middle of the island, trying to make some sense of
the tenuous spaces formed around it. Their long building
on the other side of the causeway juts out into the water.
It belongs to the warehouses formally, geographically and
metaphorically and also to the new mega-blocks. It also
refers to the scale of the port complex through sheer size
and by rejecting all play of window types, balconies and
recesses in favour of a single type of opening. While from
afar the forms may seem uncompromising, they are
actually carved and manipulated as the particular situation
demands. The ground floor of the courtyard building,
for instance, steps back on its eastern side to make way
for a narrow street. The length of the long house is
broken up on both sides to divide it into three parts. The
windows on each floor slide half a brick's length out of
alignment, a very subtle stroke that makes the entire
façade appear to vibrate slightly and thus be less stable
than at first glance.

Commercial centre,
Lucerne
[opposite] The façade
facing the church.

[below] The urban
ensemble of church,
market and hotel.

Commercial centre,
Lucerne
[below] The rhythm of
solid and transparent,
open and closed.

Ground-floor plan [oppo-
site, top right] and upper-
floor plan [opposite,
top left].
[opposite, below] Alley-
way and entrance.

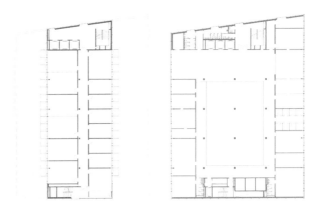

'Town planning attains its true purpose in those situations when it can bring order to a place with one house,' says Roger Diener, expressing an attitude that can be well seen in their commercial centre in Lucerne. The brief was to rationalize a prominent, grand but jumbled nineteenth-century hotel and to place a supermarket, offices and an adult education centre in its former back courtyard. The site is also next to a basilica and on a narrow shopping street. So the programme had to be monumental but at the same time precisely inserted. It adopts the same siting and form, with a central nave and two aisles, as the basilica, making a secular counterpoint. It is then uniformly wrapped in weathered green copper. Although not in a regular rhythm, the windows are set in the same plane and sized according to the scale of the metal sheets. The effect is to make the scale ambiguous, and indeed the building, with five storeys above and below ground, appears smaller than it is.

The complexities of the contemporary European city are nowhere more extreme than in Berlin, and Diener & Diener tackle those issues in a typically precise and bold way for the extension to the Swiss Embassy. The building is a late-nineteenth-century villa in a block in a once-elegant part of the city that now stands alone. The tension between traditional urban form and isolated object is what drives the architects' approach and is heightened by making the extension as unlike the existing part as possible.

The thin façade of the nineteenth-century villa, now isolated in the centre of Berlin, and the more volumetric addition.

Swiss Embassy, Berlin,
Germany
[right] Floor plan with
walled garden.
[below] Rear façade with
German Parliament in the
background.

[opposite, left] Corner of
the addition showing the
entrance.
[opposite, right] The
interior of the entrance
void at night.

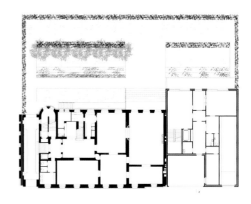

Swiss Embassy, Berlin,
Germany
[below] View from interior
into the rear garden.

[opposite] The courtyard
or void behind the new
façade's entrance.

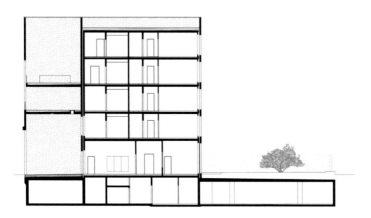

Swiss Embassy, Berlin,
Germany
[opposite, top] Cross
section showing the
entry void and the floors
behind it.

[opposite, below] The side
façade's ghostly presence
in what was once a neigh-
bourhood of villas.
[below] The calm, land-
scaped rear view.

The static nature of the bourgeois villa is underscored by
the asymmetry of the extension. The neoclassical language
of the villa is rejected, but more profoundly, the extension
is about volume and form, not surface, as the deep forecourt, the punched openings, the hint at the scale of the
space behind the wall and the metamorphosis of entry to
atrium all attest. In effect, the extension is a free-standing
building although attached to the original.

Our pluralist societies create cities with different kinds of
order. Diener & Diener accept and even celebrate this
diversity. They work with the idea of small orders, to
which their buildings respond in subtle and refined ways.
They like to focus on the spaces between buildings and
their quiet forms can be placed in configurations (Martin
Steinman calls them constellations) such as to generate
something greater and indeed urban. They use simple volumes not to create geometrically rigid urban structures,
but to make figures in space in the modern sense. The
stark language and reduced formal vocabulary, the sugges-
tion of accuracy and an economy of means all mark a
sophisticated understanding of the complicated nature
of contemporary European urbanism.

Gigon & Guyer

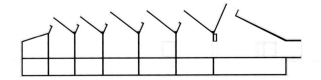

Liner Museum, Appenzell
[pp.112–13] The building sits between town and countryside.
[opposite] The concrete entry protrudes through the steel skin.

[left] Cross section.
[below] View from town along the museum's side.

While a dizzying array of themes in architecture has reached at least temporary prominence over the last twenty years, the two most notable preoccupations have been form and skin. The latter has been categorized as either applied and figurative or artistic and abstract, the former as either minimalist or exuberantly sculptural. It is easy now to see how unsatisfactory these dichotomies have been, even as we admit that they are not mere journalistic fabrications. Confusingly, the work of Gigon & Guyer has been described as each of the above, although it is actually all of them together. As striking and singular as their work is, it typically starts on the most rational premises and keeps circling in on itself so that form, material and colour are driven by each other into an ever tighter whole. This can be readily seen in the Liner Museum.

The commission for the museum came from a private art collector who wanted to exhibit the work of two local artists, Carl Liner and his son. The collection itself is modest and much cherished by local people. For this purpose the architects have designed an appropriately low-tech, low-maintenance and low-budget building. They began, sensibly enough, with the art itself by designing a single gallery room that gave an intimate experience for the viewer of the artists' small paintings and drawings. The basic form of the building is a box, developed from a group of boxes, and it is rational, economical and contextual. All of that is sensible and ordinary enough,

Liner Museum, Appenzell
Light enters the building
through the entrance, large
end window and skylights.

Liner Museum, Appenzell
[opposite, left] A framed window sits on the steel shingles.
[opposite, right] Interior of the gallery.

[below] The reading room has a large window looking back towards the railway station.

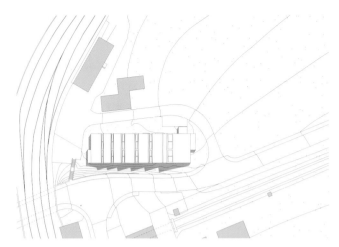

Liner Museum, Appenzell
Site plan [left] and floor
plan [opposite].

[below] Interior of foyer
with view of the landscape.

but the architects have typically pushed and pulled, questioned and distorted such rational beginnings until they develop into something new.

The architects divide the basic plan into six galleries, but the central structural wall is placed off-centre to create rooms that are either 5.75 or 7.2 metres wide. A traditional enfilade is distorted by the non-aligned placement of doorways and by two windows. The room on the northern end, in the middle of the promenade, protrudes towards the railway station and brings the tomato-red railway carriages visually into the white spaces. The vestibule on the other end of the building is much longer than the galleries, has an outsized window looking out towards the mountains and, with the only skylight facing south, feels completely different from the evenly lit, inward-looking galleries.

This subtle spatial and experiential complexity is taken up and pushed in the building's form and cladding. Appenzell is an achingly picturesque town in a beautiful landscape of soft mountains, but the actual site for the building is a contemporary mishmash of pastures, parking lots, light industry and housing on the other side of the railway from the tourist town. The building's saw-tooth roof and metal skin suggest the modesty of an industrial shed, but the metal also alludes to the local tradition of buildings sheathed in very small wood shingles

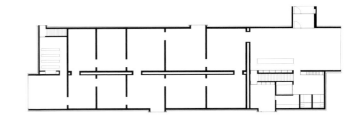

Susenbergstrasse apartment buildings, Zurich
[left] The differently coloured three blocks are villas and apartment buildings.

[below] Typical floor plan showing the blocks' close resemblance.

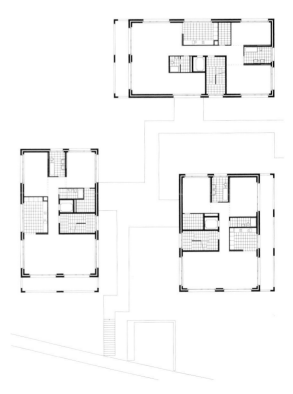

Susenbergstrasse apartment buildings, Zurich
[opposite, below and opposite, top left] The courtyard space formed by the three buildings.

[opposite, top right] The soft green edge around the housing.
[below] The harder, man-made entry space.
[right] Cross section.

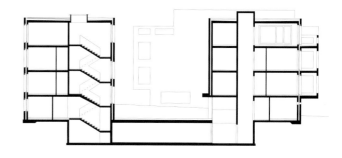

that weather to a silver grey. The form is squat as if fixed to the ground but the profile of the roof is anything but static. It is as if the building is straining against its apparent uniformity of form and skin. Indeed, the inside is distorting the form, like something trying to push its way out, as the treatment of the windows and entry suggest. This effect is not expressionist but the result of the way in which the form and skin have been generated. Because the walls of the galleries retain the same height throughout and the floor area and the angle of the roofs are kept constant, the ridge of the roof changes height, marching towards the entrance. The frankly odd form is then heightened and made more complex. The large stainless-steel panels literally fold around the roof line to avoid the articulation of a silhouette in favour of plasticity. Because each south-facing eave is divided into whole units (of three or four) the shingles are actually different sizes because of their regular pattern, relationship to the form and material qualities, though this is at first difficult to detect.

In the Liner Museum, then, we see how issues of planning, space, form, materiality and meaning are developed, and that the relationship among those constituent elements is finely balanced. This ambition for the difficult whole defines their work. Their first building, the Kirchner Museum Davos (1992), showed the same principles, though less markedly. Annette Gigon and Mike Guyer had known each other from university and had gone to work

Kalkriese Archaeological
Museum Park, Osnabrück,
Germany
[opposite and right] The
entrance building to the

park barely touches the
ground and functions as
a gateway.

with then emerging practices: Gigon with the architect and Le Corbusier scholar Arthur Rüegg and afterwards Herzog & de Meuron; Guyer with Rem Koolhaas and OMA. Each had a small practice when they decided jointly to enter the competition for the Kirchner Museum in Davos. Not only did they win the competition and build it, but the museum was hailed as a seminal work and was extensively copied. It is an exquisite synthesis of form, function, materiality and meaning. The two kinds of spaces, galleries and circulation, are differentiated materially, in lighting and from the exterior in form. The colourful and expressionist paintings of Ernst Ludwig Kirchner (1880–1938) are set off by the apparent rationality of the architecture, which in truth pays homage to the art. Kirchner went to Davos, as had so many, for medical reasons though in his case not for the recuperative effects of the mountain air. Glass has of course traditionally been used metaphorically for its transparency, but in the museum it is used in every possible way, as exterior cladding, as diffuser, as windows, even as ballast on the roof, where its sparkle can be easily seen by guests at the grand hotel near by, not to mention by skiers on the mountains.

The sudden success the architects achieved with their first building brought with it opportunities, and for a while Gigon & Guyer seemed destined to be museum architects. They built four museums and entered competitions

for another eight between 1989 and 1999, and thereby developed a position on that building type that defied style. Their latest museum, while every bit as precise as their other work, stretches them yet further. The Kalkriese Archaeological Museum Park, Osnabrück, Germany, marks the site of a legendary defeat of the Romans by Hermann (or Arminius) the Cheruskan in AD 9. There is, however, very little remaining physical evidence of this now mythical battle and archaeological investigations are ongoing. Here then is an important place that cannot be understood through the existence of objects. Gigon & Guyer, with the Swiss landscape architects Zulauf, Seitpel und Schweingruber, turn this to their advantage by eschewing the current practice of historicizing reconstruction or 'Disneyfication' in favour of a strategy that facilitates reflection and encourages imagination.

The south edge of the site is replanted to reproduce the former forest edge; to the north the forest is partially cleared to convey a sense of the openness of the former moorland and is left as a meadow. Within this creative reconstruction are three systems of circulation, which collapse historical and temporal uses. The location and assumed height of the former Teutonic earth rampart and its palisades are demarcated by vertical steel bars spaced one metre apart. The possible routes of the Teutons through the forest are demarcated by wood-chip paths. The Roman route echoes the cladding material for

Gigon & Guyer   127

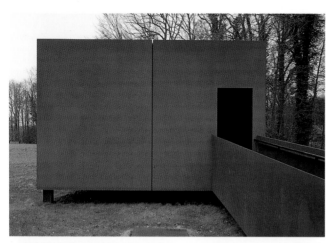

the buildings, with iron plates laid on the ground. A third system, marking current agricultural use, allows visitors to switch between the Roman and the Teutonic sides and explore freely. There is one small area that is more literal, imparting a sense of what the landscape was like in AD 9. It is a 200-square-metre hole behind rusty steel-sheet piling, which has a reconstructed rampart, a dense stand of beech and oak trees symbolizing the woods on the Teutonic side and moorland and sandy ground on the Roman side. Excavated artefacts are presented in the entrance building, which also has a tower for orientation.

Three pavilions similar in size and also clad in iron sheets are laid out on this agricultural grid. Each is devoted to heightening a particular activity or sense: 'Seeing', 'Listening' and 'Questioning'. They are, in effect, magnifying devices to facilitate reconstruction for the individual visitor. 'Seeing' is a camera obscura with a large oculus on the façade, providing a real but also altered image of what is outside. 'Listening' spouts a large steel hearing trumpet. It channels sounds into the soundproof pavilion and can be rotated by the listener in the direction of any sound. 'Questioning' sits near the end of the iron path and contains a video installation showing current world troublespots, relating the present to this ancient battle; horizontal slits are cut out of the plates to allow a visual connection. The architecture strikes a careful balance between whole and part,

Kalkriese Archaeological
Museum Park, Osnabrück,
Germany
[opposite, top left] One
of the three pavilions scattered through the park.
[opposite, top right] One
of the presumed historic
routes demarcated by
steel panels.

[opposite, below] The
'Listening' pavilion at
the forest's edge.
The entrance building
and its observation tower
[below] and façade [right].

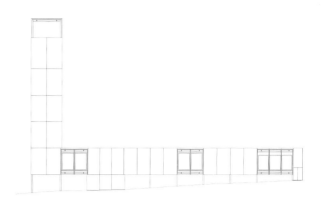

Pflegiareal housing and offices, Zurich [below] View from the street.

The pedestrian entrance [opposite, below] leads to the courtyard [opposite, top].

representation and abstraction, the familiar and the new, the past and the present.

What Gigon & Guyer like about designing museums is working with understanding clients and designing for a concentrated gaze. But their way of working and their architectural stance, which takes account of things that are neither good nor bad but rather more or less suited to the task, can be applied to any building type. Indeed, they have worked on quite a bit of housing, where the room for formal or personal expression is relatively constrained; where, in other words, the architect needs to be especially rigorous and clever in order to be inventive. Their house interiors tend to be restrained, sharing a neutrality with their museum buildings, which analogously allows one's life to be at the centre. With housing they often collaborate with artists and have evolved a distinctive approach to colour. As they put it, architects need to work with artists for the same reason as they work with engineers: for their expertise.

The three apartment buildings on the Susenbergstrasse in Zurich are in an exclusive area on the hill overlooking the lake. They are designed for wealthy singles or couples and are flexible and generous spatially. The plans are practically organized around a central core of vertical circulation, bathrooms and kitchens creating spaces on either side. The siting, fenestration and use of colour,

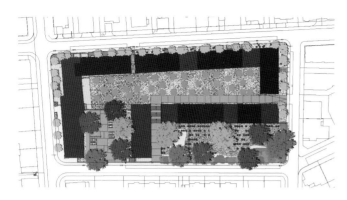

Pflegiareal housing and offices, Zurich
Site plan [left] and long section [opposite].

[below] The landscaped inner courtyard.

however, are provocative. Breaking the building mass into three volumes brings them to the scale of the single-family houses and villas in the area. But in contrast to those solitary masses, these three houses must respond to each other in their organization, fenestration and proportion. Although not identical they are similar in mass, and it is as if the individual buildings were placed on the site and then rotated until the best mutual orientation was achieved. Each floor has windows on all four sides (thus kitchens and bathrooms have windows). The loggias, which run along the south, east or west side, are variously placed.

The play between whole and part that characterized the Liner Museum is explored here with form and applied colour. The colour scheme was designed in collaboration with the artist Adrian Schiess, with whom they have worked before. His work involves laying huge sheets of colour in existing buildings. Here, though, the colour is not simply applied as an additional element but is added to the concrete outer layer to achieve a powder-like effect that allows the sense of concrete to come through. Each building is done in a single pastel – lemon yellow, grey-green or apricot – with only the western side painted blue.

At the Pflegiareal housing and offices Gigon & Guyer deal with a complex urban site of new and existing buildings in

a mixed programme. But here too they achieve a balance between rationality and expressiveness. The existing 1930s buildings to the west are offices, while the new ones to the east are primarily housing. The apartments are so designed that they can be rented with traditional space divisions or a minimum of rooms. The architects wanted to retain the spatial character of the complex, a former hospital, and so the new buildings oscillate between a closed block structure and single volumes. Large openings are used to confuse the distinction between mass and skeleton and to lend the buildings the appropriate character. Colour here is used not to help articulate the masses but to define the enclosed spaces. Consequently, only the surface is coloured and not the depth, as the raw concrete of the window reveals shows. One façade is blue, one white towards the courtyard and the other a bright yellow-green. Colour is also used in contrast to the cool, almost neutral architectural language and lush backdrop of trees and gardens.

Marcel Meili, Markus Peter Architekten

RiffRaff 2, Zurich
[pp. 134–35] The new building stands on the corner with RiffRaff 1 behind.

[below] Cinema entrance on the right under the canopy, restaurant and bar to the left and flats above. [opposite] Cinema and submerged foyer.

The last twenty years in architecture have been a period of tumult, with more than the usual number of 'isms' vying for primacy at the same time as radical changes to building procurement have changed the nature of the profession. Since founding their practice in 1987 Marcel Meili and Markus Peter have been looking for ways to react to the increasingly dynamic nature of building production, its anonymous clients, open and changing programme and increasingly complex project structure. Responses pursued elsewhere have included disposable architecture or systems that were quick and/or flexible. But Marcel Meili, Markus Peter Architekten evolved a more complex response, which also asserts the necessity of the architect. They looked for what is essential, what will literally remain, no matter what changes to the design or, indeed, to the building larger forces may impose. This explains their particular synthesis of space, structure and site. While they insist that as designers what matters ultimately is the physical artefact – what the door handle looks and feels like, what the proportion of something is – their work is driven by a highly intelligent, inquisitive engagement with the totality of architecture.

Once it is no longer axiomatic to make space, structure and site the force behind design, the results may be quite radical. The bridge at Murau (with Jürg Conzett) is emblematic of their ambitions. In it the beam is the bridge is the material is the space. Even with a bridge they are

RiffRaff 2, Zurich
[opposite] Interior of the complex.

[below] Interior of bar and restaurant.
[right] Ground-floor plan.

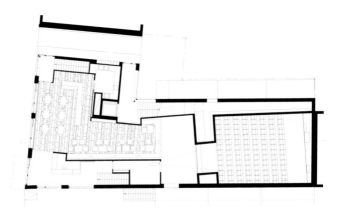

not interested in a tectonically expressive structural system or a formal gesture but for all architectural issues to synchronize. At the Hyatt Hotel in Zurich they are building, for example, the structure defines a spatial and material concept, which establishes an order that cannot be changed. This has proven useful in dealing with the clients over the protracted design and construction process.

This interest in space and structure is met by an engagement with materials and urban design. Meili recounts that when he lectured on elementary statics at the applied arts school in Zurich it made him return to and reconsider first principles. But equally important was the centrality of the city that Aldo Rossi brought to the students at ETH. Here too Meili and Peter have taken the lessons and developed them. Instead of the Italian city of history they accept the fragmentation and collage of the modern city. The issue then becomes not urban design per se, but how to respond to the cultural and economic organization of a new kind of urban life. One can see the powerful outcome of these concerns in their roof extension to Zurich's main railway station (with Axel Fickert and Kaschka Knapkiewicz). It must fulfil a simple function, but one that is given metropolitan dimensions. They thought Zurich should have the kind of urban theatre that great cities have, so they bring together the space of the trains, of the city and of the pedestrians. The outsized roof leans out into the city on huge canted columns; at night it

RiffRaff 2, Zurich
[right] Living area.
[opposite] Bedroom
and bathroom on court-
yard side.

displays the trains behind a metal screen. The structure necessary to do this is sophisticated but hidden, and the timber cladding incongruous but effective.

At the Swiss Re Rüschlikon Centre for Global Dialogue just above Lake Zurich the various issues come together in a complex of buildings. The client, a wealthy and powerful reinsurance company, wanted a centre where people from the worlds of finance, science, politics and culture would convene to examine developments and trends that might be of significance for the global risk community. The main architectural idea is the way one moves around the site, or its urban design. The architects were taken by the story behind the existing 1920s, French-style villa. It is oriented north–south, as is typical in the then owner's home canton of Bern, where houses face the Jungfrau; every other house on Lake Zurich is oriented east–west to face the water. This story and their brief for the centre as a kind of think-tank led Meili and Peter away from giving the lake predominance and instead to gathering discrete objects around a central space and controlling the view. There are five distinct parts to the building: places of contemplation (main building), of dining, of gazing (the romantic object in the landscape), of chatting (a bar) and of managing (the original villa).

The main building is a bar form, which, although much larger than the original villa, nestles unobtrusively into a

hillock; its entrance under a cantilevered roof is discreet. From the entrance one can slip directly upstairs to the luxurious if austere bedrooms, thought of as monks' cells. But most of the building is a collection of informal meeting spaces to invite conversation and reflection – niches, sports facilities, a restaurant and a library; there are only three actual seminar rooms. From the foyer one begins the promenade through the park. The massive, exposed, black concrete piers of the entrance hall give way to columns as the topography and the building's section dip down and put the visitor in the trees. In this far corner the plan and section finally open up to allow a view of the lake and the central space. Here the structure switches to huge pre-stressed and cantilevered glulam (glued and laminated) beams, which recall the branches of a tree. They seem to sit on huge expanses of glass. The fitness room, sauna and library are below on the garden level, from which a colonnade of concrete, cast with crushed black, green and clear glass, on the west side of the grounds, leads one around to the original villa. Attached to it is a building with a bar and dining room and a view towards the lake. Just below the level of the garden, by the shore of the lake, winds a path to a small tea-house. Near the foyer, to which one returns, is an after-hours-type bar in a former garage.

The sheer inventiveness of the structure and of the materials used is staggering. For example, there are

Swiss Re Rüschlikon
Centre for Global Dialogue,
Zurich
[opposite, top left] Park
end of the long building.
[opposite, top right]
Elevation only hinting at
the library and lecture
space behind it.

[opposite, below] The
façades of the bedrooms.
[below] The long building
nestling into the hillock
from under the entry
canopy.

144   Swiss Made

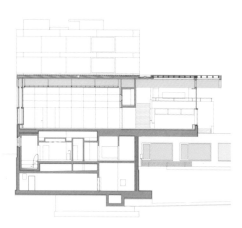

Swiss Re Rüschlikon
Centre for Global Dialogue,
Zurich
[p.144, top] The long entry
hall with examples of furniture by Adolf Krischanitz
and Hermann Czech.

[p.144, below] The double-
height room in the trees at
the end of the corridor.
[p.144–45] The long building stepping down towards
the lake.

Swiss Re Rüschlikon
Centre for Global Dialogue,
Zurich
[opposite, top] Cross
section through the
double-height space.

[opposite, below] The
dining room and the
original villa.
[below] Site plan.

twenty-two types of concrete used; the finish on the walls is mostly *Kalk*, not plaster, a very old technique which is remarkably hard and flat; the ceiling in the main building is a very fine bronze mesh behind which services are hidden. The result, however, is not fussy but bold and rich. The architects are well aware that they are working at the end of one of the last cultures that can still build well. They are keen to exercise the possibilities in such craftsmanship through an interest in the material itself, in how it can be worked and made beautiful. The intellectual issue is how to keep architecture physical, how to express a material aura when architecture has become dematerialized through hybrids, new ways of combining materials and the organization of the construction process. Material expression for Meili and Peter is not a moral or conceptual issue but a physical one.

They enjoy working with other architects, developing their architecture through dialogue. Such an openness to others' propositions was behind their decision not to design new furniture for the Rüschlikon centre. Instead, it was custom-made by the Viennese architects Adolf Krischanitz and Hermann Czech; it is luxurious and often blatantly decorative, and works well in the building's forceful and unified spaces. Architecture and nature are again brought together in their competition entry for the Swiss Embassy in Washington, DC. Meili and Peter rejected the idea of the embassy as the ambassador's villa and

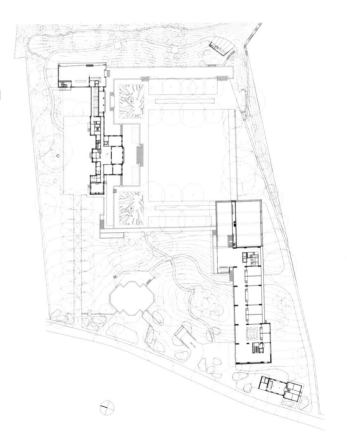

Parasite House,
Rotterdam, the Netherlands
[below and opposite, top left]
House on the canal during
the day and at night.

[opposite, top right] House
from the street side.
[opposite, below] The
temporary nature of the
construction.

Marcel Meili, Markus Peter Architekten 149

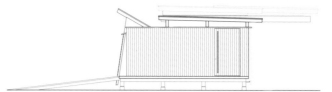

**Parasite House,
Rotterdam, the Netherlands**
[left] Side elevation.
[below] The narrow spaces
under the flipped-up roof
and the larger workspace
under the flat roof.
[opposite] The long wall
with its hexagonal cut-outs.

understood it as a kind of theatre. They thus made a complete separation between public and private functions, the former being placed on a plinth enclosed by a glass wall with movable interior partitions. The residence literally sits above this, a series of trusses in the trees that divide the space into four flats with courtyards. The roof is covered with moss, the terraces enclosed by shrubs, and a single large window in each flat punches through the greenery. Nature is developed as a concept of form and not from a neo-romantic ecological view that denies the character of contemporary life.

The RiffRaff cinema and bar is an earlier project by Meili and Peter, which they are now extending. It is situated in Kreis 5, a former industrial and working-class quarter with the highest concentration of different ethnic groups in the city. As elsewhere, as industry has moved out, culture and an alternative scene have moved in. The first stage, RiffRaff 1 (1997–98), involved converting a late-nineteenth-century building that had variously housed a sequence of theatres and finally a billiards hall and amusement arcade into an independent art-house cinema. Economically and socially, the programme for RiffRaff 1 needed two screens and a bar, which is dense relative to the floor area. The logical position for the projection room meant that one of the beams of light from the projector would cross over the bar area. While this created formidable technical problems owing to the low light intensity

of film, the architects were enchanted by a beautiful mental image from Italian cinema, that of the projected image flickering on cigarette smoke. The architects characteristically brought these programmatic and technical issues together, creating a kinetic, filmic environment of light, sound, people, space and smoke. Technically the bar needed to be quite dark in order not to interfere with the projected light passing through it, and a black box suited the brief as well. The optical issues were studied by means of large mock-ups including projectors and smoke machines. Some of these studies yielded unexpected results. For instance, a sheet of glass was the obvious way to insulate sound from the theatre while allowing the projection to enter it. It would not adversely affect the quality of the image, but did need to be angled slightly to avoid reflections in the cinema. This has the lovely effect, though, of a faint image of the film being reflected on to the bar's ceiling. With RiffRaff 1 the architects transformed function into atmosphere.

The addition to RiffRaff (with Astrid Staufer and Thomas Hasler) extends the original building to the corner and adds two cinemas, a bistro and flats above. The cinema and restaurant are as atmospheric as in the original, and with the flats achieve a barely stable dialogue between the nineteenth and twentieth centuries. In the façade one sees the idea of a traditional wall, with openings as voids, as well as the modern idea of the wall dissolved, of

Marcel Meili, Markus Peter Architekten   151

Swiss Embassy,
Washington, DC, USA
[right] Ground-floor plan.
[below] Transparent
ground floor and green
upper floor.
[opposite] Roof plan.

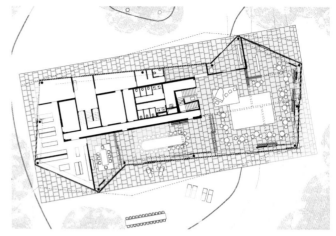

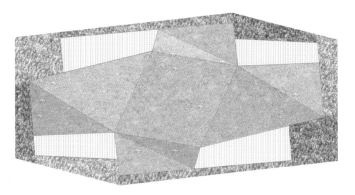

a mere skeleton or grid. The flats exhibit a similar tension. The architects opened up the nineteenth-century syntax of rooms and enfilades to allow spaces to flow into each other without losing the privacy of rooms, zones and cells. They wanted huge windows, but on the interior these all have a lintel or a parapet and so again belong to both worlds. The façade works to mitigate the power of the big windows to make a big statement. Its palette is based on the brightly coloured buildings in the area – sienna red, orange yellow, powder blue or pea green – but here the colours are muted, with a top layer applied over the first coat to tone it down, using a technique developed by the practice. The effect is of a very fine piece of weaving and again displays an ambivalence towards the wall. Only in the window frames, the ground floor and the interior are the colours used as boldly as in the surrounding buildings.

In summer 2001 the Meili and Peter practice had its first retrospective, at the Architecture Museum in Basel, and were themselves surprised to discover that their concerns had not really changed very much over the years, the chief of them being space. They have, however, developed in terms of their ability to bring the issues of structures, urban design and materials together in equal measure to produce a complex whole. These issues and their continual development can be clearly seen in their Parasite House, Rotterdam. It is a portable modest and inexpensive wood building for odd and temporary sites,

based on an unbuilt project of theirs from 1989, in which every piece is an infinitely adaptable whole. It has no fixed foundation, merely sitting on concrete beams, and is constructed of large, self-supporting wooden sheets that are easily transportable. This allows the floor, roof and walls to be treated identically, almost as a modularized monolith. Thus the characteristic legibility of timber construction and of a house is suppressed and the architecture becomes abstract. There are not even recognizable doors or windows. This innovation in construction and the use of materials is typical of Meili and Peter, and is driven not by sculptural interests or a desire to dematerialize or lend a material new meaning. Rather, they seek to investigate the properties of a material that develop under different spatial, structural and/or constructional conditions.

Peter Märkli

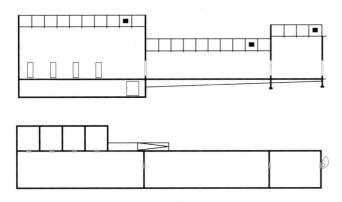

The pervasiveness of media culture can make Le Corbusier's dictum that architecture is a patient search seem rather quaint.

Peter Märkli's increasing renown, however, is built on just such disciplined and steady development. Märkli had, for his generation, an unfashionable interest in buildings regardless of their period or pedigree. In his early work his engagement with Italian architecture's highly evolved formal complexities is clear, as is his understanding of its juxtaposition of such basic elements as the wall and openings and of its strategies of balance and tension. His work from this period typically has a clear distinction between the front, which is often figurative, and the sides and back. There is a strong play on axiality and symmetry, often skewed by the careful placement of a sculpture or column. Form and façade often dictate the organization of the interior. As Märkli says, 'I wasn't looking for a style but for a means of expression. Since I was culturally at level zero, this expression could only be something very basic.'

His best-known work to date is undoubtedly La Congiunta, a small museum to display the sculptures of Hans Josephsohn. It is a long, silent building placed in a vineyard next to a railway embankment, a motorway and a riverbed in the stony landscape of Ticino. The architecture is driven by a profound understanding of the sculptures, which are

La Congiunta,
Giornico, Ticino
[pp.154–55] Entry side
of the building and the
vineyard.
Long section [opposite,
top] and ground-floor
plan [opposite, middle].

[opposite, below] The final
gallery space.
[below] The middle gallery
with a lowered roof.
[p.158] The raw concrete.
[p.159] The side of the
building, showing how it
steps in section.

Single-family house,
Hünenberg
Main living space with its
large paving slabs and view
from atop the hill.

highly plastic and combine essentially figurative elements. They express mass rather than surface and tackle issues of the perception of weight.

The building perfectly demonstrates how his engagement with the fundamentals of architecture has developed. It is almost pure architecture, a concrete spatial container without insulation or services. Its form seems to be the direct result of its space as it steps in section in response to developments in the art. The plan is organized around an axis that runs off-centre through three long spaces with four small rooms off the last one. It is toplit. Märkli is here working with the most elemental architectural devices only, namely proportion, space, light, materiality and programme. The raw concrete bears every trace of its fabrication. The museum is not, however, an exemplar of a now fashionable minimalism nor does it assert the moral implications once associated with this term. Rather, it simply strips out everything that is unnecessary to the task at hand.

La Congiunta is also important because of Märkli's personal relationship with the sculptor. He first went as a student to meet Josephsohn after reading a review of his work, seeking intellectual stimulation outside ETH Zurich. Josephsohn became something of a mentor to Märkli, who has incorporated his work into many of his buildings and who has the sculptor's pieces in his office and at

Single-family house, Hünenberg
[opposite] Entrance tucked under the cantilever.

[below] The front seen from the street.

home. The other important influence from his student days,
which confirms him as something of an outsider, was
the important Graubünden architect Rudolf Olgiati, who
synthesized regional characteristics such as volume
and mass with Corbusian modernism. Märkli describes his
own influences as traditional principles and the legacy
of classical modernism.

Märkli's profound engagement with architecture and
attempt to assimilate and combine what he has seen has
led him from classical devices to more topographical,
contextual and plastic concerns. The house in Ehrlenbach
is seminal, for it uses concrete both as mass and as
planes. Houses must first and foremost erect walls and
define a space without shutting the world out completely.
In the typically unspectacular social and physical landscape of the suburbs, however, it is hard to find a language
with which to do this. In Ehrlenbach the concrete walls
define a first territory, while glass walls on two sides just
inside them enclose the domestic realm. This play between
mass and transparency is made even clearer when the
concrete walls that provide privacy for the glazed living
spaces are coloured pink and treated as screens. The
house is rectilinear and its language indeed reduced. But
it is also strongly plastic, with its interplays of light and
shadow, transparency and opacity, inside and outside.

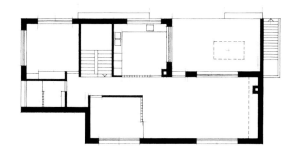

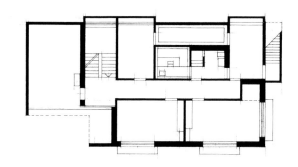

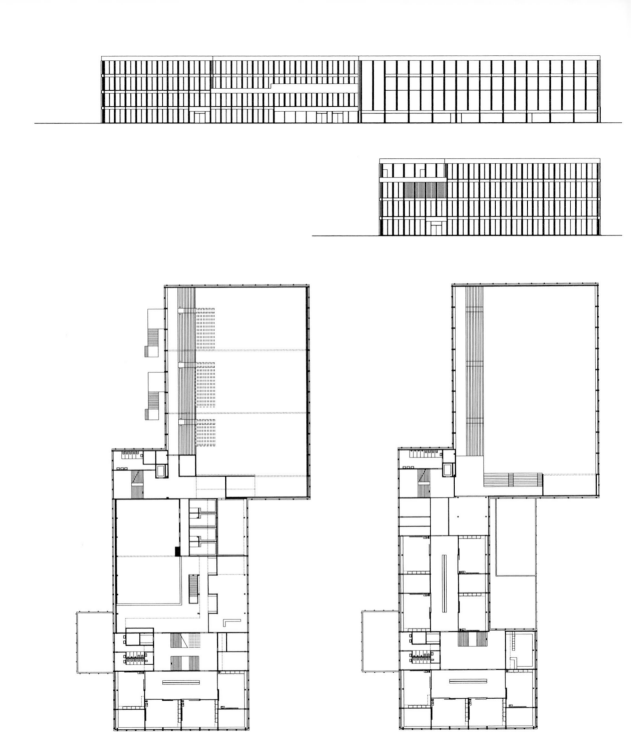

School, Zurich North
[opposite, top] Long east elevation of primary school with adjoining sports hall. [opposite, middle] West elevation of secondary school.

Plans of first level [opposite, below left] and second level [opposite, below right] of sports area, common area and primary school.

The single-family house in Azmoos shows Märkli's fundamental interests developing into increasing sophistication. The building, which sits on a plain, looks symmetrical and T-shaped from one side, but the form is actually a more plastic one of solids and voids, positives and negatives. The entrance façade has a single squarish window placed almost in the centre, with a cantilevered upper storey the entire length. At ground level it is divided almost evenly between the void of the garage and the solid of the house. Märkli gives the house just enough axiality and symmetry to impart a sense of it without fully achieving it.

The first floor is private, with rooms organized off a long corridor that can be used for any number of functions. On the top floor the form pushes out in both directions and the plan is freer though it still retains a sense of individual rooms. The master bedroom is gently separated from the living area; the kitchen, typically for Märkli, is glazed to make it part of the living space. The staircase does not hug an exterior wall but becomes space-defining. The terrace, which on the lower floor is long, on this floor claws out some of the interior to become both long and deep, covered and open, defined by an opaque and a glazed wall, a rich spatial experience and a play of inside and outside. Because the rooms on this floor are taller than below they are also deeper. The grey and green irregular checkerboard pattern on lime plaster further softens the perception of the form, confuses the house's

scale and shifts the wall away from any notions of naturalism. This formal and spatial manipulation does not feel at all mannered.

The single-family house in Hünenberg is based on organizational principles similar to the one in Azmoos, but its form is dictated by the hillside on which it sits. The way we actually live is reflected in the wide asphalt drive bringing the road right up to the house. The subsequent entrance sequence is, however, more indirect as one slides first sideways under a cantilever towards a white wall, through a metal door and then up a switchback stair to the living area on the topmost floor, which contains five rooms, including a large bedroom. Glass block and a glazed kitchen, the kitchen and study not quite aligned with each other and the latter with a sliding partition to the sitting room all help break down the identity of the rooms. The sitting room is stretched across the house, with one side facing the valley and the other leading to an outdoor room defined by two massive walls and the house's roof. There is a visual connection from the valley on one side of the house through the sitting room and the outdoor room across the narrow terrace that runs the length of the house along the hill at the back. Binding the house to the earth is the dark umber pigment of its lime plaster. The floors are covered in large red concrete slabs 2 x 2 metres with 1.5 cm joints between them to give them a decorative aspect.

Single-family house,
Azmoos
[opposite] Front and
side façades.

[below] Approach from
the street.
[right] Cross section.

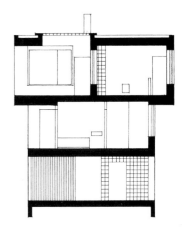

Single-family house, Azmoos

[below left] Side elevation facing the street approach. [below right] Detail of garage that goes through to the rear.

[from left to right] Ground-, first- and top-floor plans. [opposite, below] Rear façade's play of solid and void, protrusion and recession.

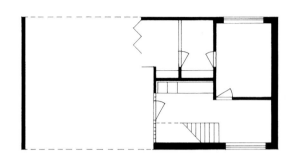

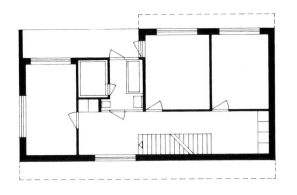

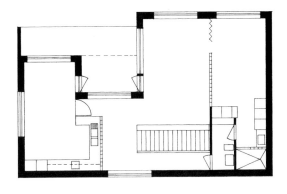

The school in Oerlikon on the edge of Zurich is by far Märkli's largest commission to date, but formally adopts the same themes he has been working on for twenty-five years. The brief is for a kindergarten, primary and secondary schools, sports hall, library and dining area. Planning regulations stipulate that new buildings conform to the existing height and block pattern, but because this is a former industrial area the site and the masses are quite large. The problem of the plan's consequent depth is solved by dispersing the programme into different buildings with generous amounts of glazing that are then gathered on a concrete plinth. A large outdoor space can be shared by all groups. Classes are grouped by year and each part of the school has its own territory. Two or three classrooms are clustered in a pedagogical experiment where teachers share responsibility for them. There are no corridors since the means of egress in the case of fire is directly from each classroom. The common area in front of them can thus be fully glazed and assume multiple functions. The same windows are used throughout.

Although Märkli built little in the first ten years of his career he was far from idle – observing, learning, drawing. He works both from his own studio and in collaboration with the architect Gody Kühnis. Märkli's is an architecture of resistance that insists it is still an art and has inherent, unmediated value.

Miller & Maranta

Market hall, Aarau
[pp.172–73] View of the
outdoor space that is
linked to the main square.
[below] View from one of
the alleyways.

[opposite, top] The wall
perceived as open and
closed.
[opposite, below] Elevation
on the main square.

Internationally famous Basel practices such as Herzog & de Meuron and Diener & Diener bestride their small home city like giants. Add to this that the region also boasts buildings by such famous architects as Tadao Ando, Frank O. Gehry, Zaha Hadid, Renzo Piano and Alvaro Siza, and one can imagine how difficult it may be for a young firm to establish itself. Miller & Maranta have been quietly winning competitions and building small projects since 1989, biding their time for that big project that will bring them renown.

Their patient and steady advance comes in part from their theoretical position as unabashed students of Fabio Reinhart and Miroslav Sik, who developed Aldo Rossi's idea of the analogical city. This school of thought postulates that things that are truly immanent can be understood only by their re-imagining. Images are not regarded as archetypes but as analogies, firmly grounded in our own memories and in the collective specificity of what exists. For the architect this theory entails the difficult task of interrogating our daily and unspectacular built environment for its subtle poetry and finding an analogous way to represent it. In short, what is the physicality that is conjured up by a feeling, memory or experience and how can it be represented?

Working within the theory of an analogue architecture requires precision and subtlety to prevent it from

Market hall, Aarau
[below] The rhythm, regu-
larity and effects of the
fence-like construction.

[right] Site plan.
[opposite] The interior's
single column.

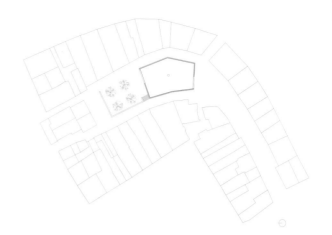

degenerating into nostalgia. It is hard work for the architect
and often for the user or viewer too, for it eschews facile
exuberance of form and material. The Volta Schoolhouse
in Basel, Miller & Maranta's first major building, is a good
example of this need to look closely and to work rigorously,
for at first glance it could be dismissed as the taut, minimal box so often characterized as Swiss architecture.

Yet even from the outside the building mediates complexities. The site, a 6.2-metre hole left over from
demolition of one third of the still contiguous fuel depot,
seems unpropitious for a schoolhouse. It is undoubtedly
contemporary in its complexity, surrounded by a motorway on one side, an industrial quarter on the other, a
power station with an extremely tall chimney and nine-
teenth- and twentieth-century housing stock. Moreover,
it had to be built quickly and inexpensively.

One of the fundamental tenets of analogue architecture
is that the building should look as if it belongs there as a
matter of course. And the school's massing, site plan and
concrete façades, with large, regular, aluminium windows
set to the outside, do refer to the industrial character of
the area. In fact, it rises even taller than the fuel depot.
But the programme must also drive the architecture, and
in this case what you see is not quite what you get. The
concrete of the façade, for example, has metal oxide
added to it to give it a slight tone, marking it off from an

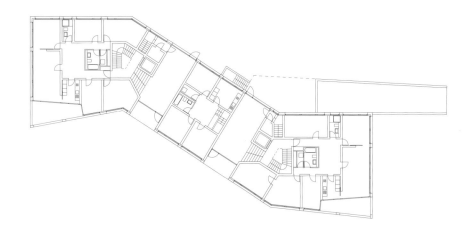

Schwarzpark apartments, Basel
[opposite, top] Ground-floor plan.
[opposite, below] The form undulates on the park side to maximize the view.
[right] The block respects the urban corner.

industrial beton brut. The placing of the windows might challenge our assumption that the concrete wall is structural. The schoolyard in front doesn't have a playing field or tarmac but with its trees, gravel and surrounding wall is school-like and relaxed. The ground-floor windows drop down to transform the corridor into a loggia to the front, literally mediating between industrial and school-house characters.

Likewise, the interior at first seems hard and abstract but the same principles are applied. The spatial organization involves a sophisticated system of lengthwise structural walls, which remove the need for space-consuming beams. The front and rear façades thus carry no load. The basement has a different structural system to contain the sports hall. Spatially there are four long strips, each of which contains classrooms and courtyards arranged in a zigzag formation. The glazed courtyards provide daylight deep into the plan, and their alternating placement means that one is always looking through these glazed voids, the views mediated by reflections, plays of solid and void, sunlight and daylight, structural walls and infill ones. With an economy of means the perceptual effect is made complex and rich, creating images and noises in the foreground and background. It is difficult to know sometimes what one is seeing where; with one's views bounced around so much it is just about possible to lose spatial orientation. The result is to create a slightly dreamlike interior atmosphere, in contrast to the apparent no-nonsense concrete exterior.

The visual disorientation is purposely and sensibly reduced for the classrooms, but here again there are subtleties that someone sitting there, day in, day out, perhaps daydreaming during a lesson, will feel and perhaps eventually recognize. The walls and ceilings at first appear simply pearl grey, in neutral light, but are actually painted with a layer of gold overlaid with one of silver in the opposite direction, done with a brush and not a roller to help create the textile-like pattern and sense of depth. The colour varies according to the weather and the season from grey to gold and silver to blue. The interior frames of the windows, unlike the exterior, are of timber. The classrooms successfully create the feel of a traditional, remembered place, and are not just well-engineered pedagogical boxes.

Miller & Maranta's theoretical position precludes a single approach, be it formal, typological or tectonic. Since each project responds to their reading of the feeling of a place and its programme, each project will be, in the largest sense, site-specific. This is clear in their project for a market hall in Aarau, a small town but also the capital of the canton and as such an important administrative and cultural centre, as well as being still something of a market town. Although the predominant material in the

Volta Schoolhouse, Basel
[below] The regular façade to the playground with a shift at ground-floor level.

[opposite, top] Side façade.
[opposite, below] Rear façade with existing fuel depot next to it.

Volta Schoolhouse, Basel
[below and opposite]
Large windows, courtyards
and surface treatments
animate the hard
circulation spaces.
[right] One of the interior
courtyards.

Volta Schoolhouse, Basel
[left] Different surface treatments of classroom and courtyard.
[below top] Floor plan at classroom level.

[below bottom] Section showing large span of sports hall underneath and rhythm of courtyards above.

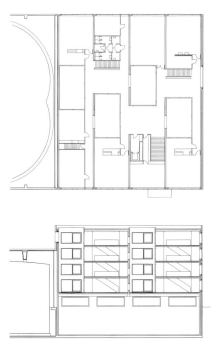

Volta Schoolhouse, Basel
[opposite, top left] The light and reflections from the courtyard seen through the wood-framed window of a classroom.

[opposite, top right] The sunken sports hall.
[opposite, below] Subtly different qualities of light are captured in a classroom.

old town is limestone from the nearby Jura region, it is typical of Miller & Maranta's interpretive approach that they proposed a light, timber construction.

As with the Volta Schoolhouse, the site plan for the market hall appears almost obvious. The form inflects according to the surrounding buildings, following them around the corner of the square. But the architects read the site as atypical for a market, instead recognizing it as a place where a warehouse or other non-public shed would normally be placed. Here too the architects had to reconcile the contradictory demands of programme and urban type. Small market halls are expected to be light and almost temporary, whereas a warehouse at its best would have the quiet dignity of just going about its business. In Aarau the architects successfully built a hall that does both those things, creating an exterior wall that is both closed and open, skin and mass, fence as well as wall. The close spacing of the regular wooden posts, along with the kink in the hall's form, makes it appear either solid or transparent, depending on where one stands. Instead of the usual interior columns there are posts and a single central column to give a free interior. It is critical structurally for torsion but is also important as a kind of echo of ancestral architectural memory. The hall is thus solid and trabeated, building and skeleton, modest-looking but sophisticated structurally.

'Schwarzpark', a complex of family apartments, again shows Miller & Maranta's disinterest in a consistent formal vocabulary, as the building snakes around for views into the neighbouring park. The floor plans are based on a Basel type. For a practice that works with memory and feelings, the images and propositions for the projects can ironically appear dry and matter-of-fact. But Miller & Maranta's architecture requires some time on the part of the occupant or viewer and a deep investigation on the part of the practice. Part of their working method, they say, is to talk a lot, in order to decipher the true agenda.

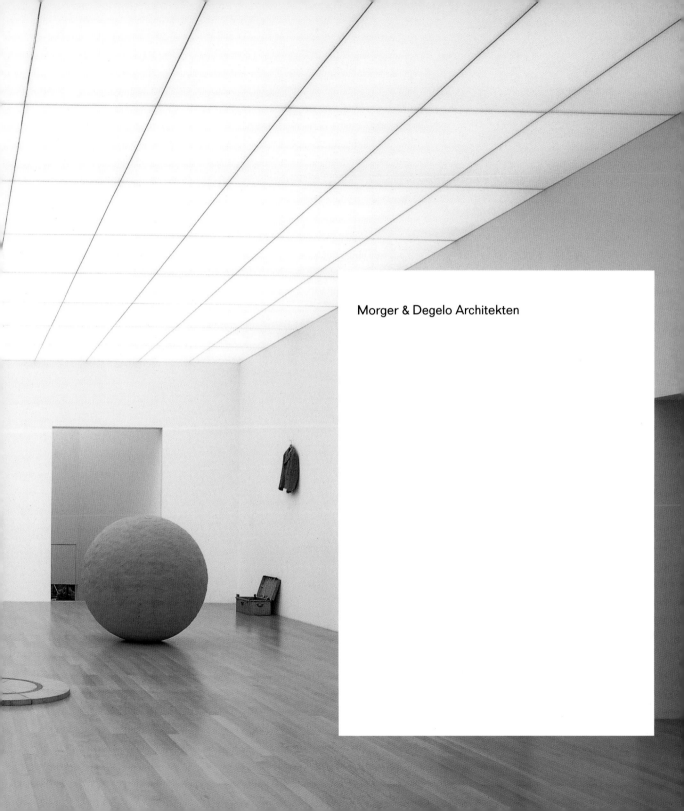

Morger & Degelo Architekten

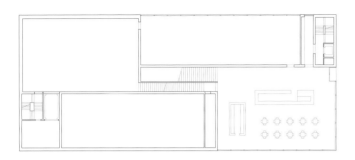

Liechtenstein Art Museum,
Vaduz
[pp.188–89] Interior of one
of the upstairs galleries.
[opposite, top] Ground-
floor plan.

[opposite, below] Entry
and main stairs leading
to upper-floor galleries.
[below] Reflections of the
surroundings in the con-
crete-and-glass wall.

The most common prejudice about contemporary Swiss architecture, that it is typified by the cool, minimal box, seems at first validated by the work of Morger & Degelo Architekten. Their buildings do have a severely reduced formal vocabulary, especially on the exterior. But this stringency only masks the ambiguous tension in their interests between context and the autonomy of form. Although they became architects via an unusual route – Morger having trained as a draughtsman, Degelo as a furniture maker – and in a city dominated by Herzog & de Meuron, they have since become among the most successful architects of their generation.

For the Art Museum in Liechtenstein, built with Christian Kerez from Zurich, Morger and Degelo begin as usual with the urban context. But Vaduz recalls Gertrude Stein's characterization of Los Angeles: 'there is no there there'. Its population is about that of a large town and its postwar prosperity derived from services and banking has given rise to a collection of generic office buildings that are uninterested in such niceties as urban design. In this unpropitious if not hostile environment, on the main thoroughfare crowded with such buildings, a site was reserved for an art museum of the largest possible volume to house a very good collection.

Faced with building a museum amid so much tat, the architects proposed a no-nonsense black box to contain

[below left] The main façade with the royal castle rising above it.
[below right] The polished and seamless concrete façade seen from the street.
[opposite] Side elevation with windows of the ground-level galleries.

St. Alban-Ring housing, Basel
[right] Upper-level floor plan.
[below] Façade facing the motorway and train tracks.
[opposite, top left] The housing has views over the park.
[opposite, top right] Facing the motorway with an intermediary space.
[opposite, below] The end of the tapering form.

a quintessential white gallery space. The black, shiny building gives almost nothing of its interior away, except when viewed from the wooded hill and prince's castle above, where the clarity and strictness of its plan can be seen in the roof lights. It is a monolith that quietly but insistently rejects its neighbours without seeming prim. The 40-cm-thick concrete walls have no joints and are almost uninterrupted by openings; where there are windows they are just large sheets of glass in the same plane as the walls and so blend in. But what makes it much more than the cliché of the black box is its physicality and craftedness. The surface is made rich by a mixed aggregate of veined gravel from the nearby Rhine, black basalt from Germany and pigment. (To achieve an even distribution of the varied aggregates the concrete had to be mixed on site.) The exterior surface of these massive walls was then ground, sanded and polished by hand by ten workers for six months. They removed 8 mm. The result is a surface that reflects the buildings around it, the sky and the weather, but because it is handcrafted and therefore not a perfectly flat surface the reflections are modulated, blurred, the surroundings transformed into something beyond themselves.

The surface itself varies greatly from a sort of mother-of-pearl to gloss black. The qualities of its surface lend the building a physical presence it could not have if it were glazed, for instance. Whereas other architects pursue

**House Müller,
Staufen, Basel**
[below] The abstract and
inward-looking form among
its suburban neighbours.
[opposite, top left] The
entry façade.

[opposite, top right] The
outdoor spaces around
the L-shaped form.
[opposite, below] The
privacy of the courtyard.

dematerialization, the form here is shiny but retains its sense of mass. Put another way, the surface treatment reveals little depth yet the form and the material suggest mass.

The exterior points up and then transforms the ephemerality of its surroundings and the interior revels in the extreme introversion of the building. Although the entire ground-floor corner by the entry is glazed and the entry pushes into the building, the door itself is opaque. But on entering the foyer you are unmistakably in the realm of art. The ticket area, bookshop, kitchen and bar are treated abstractly and are almost undifferentiated from each other. They are made of oak, as are the tables, chairs and floor. Directly in front of you is a flight of low steps up to the galleries, which have no windows but a uniform ceiling of translucent panels. These spaces are paradigmatic white boxes, varying from each other only in their proportions. (This is partly in response to the need for the building to house not only the national collection, but also selections from the prince's, as well as temporary installations.) On the floor below the galleries have a long band of windows in rooms that are otherwise identical in plan to those above but slightly lower in height. The plan is strictly organized, almost diagrammatic. A central staircase divides the area into four, with two sets of similarly sized rooms. No more reduction or humility of architecture could be achieved. The spaces can be partitioned, but

House Müller,
Staufen, Basel
[right] Ground-floor plan.
[below] The courtyard's
reflecting pool, paved patio
and wrapping windows.

[opposite] The spatial rich-
ness of the ground floor.

otherwise the architecture delivers the basics: floors, walls, space and light.

Though an extreme response to an extreme situation, the Art Museum does illustrate certain characteristics of Morger & Degelo's work. Their predilection for reduction can sometimes obscure their interest in maintaining architecture's physicality and in the craft of building. As their morphological approach to a site demonstrates, they are of a generation that starts from an acceptance of what exists. All these tendencies can be seen in their design for a centre in the town of Reinach.

The four buildings have three different programmes, which are approached individually but combine to form a loose whole. The office block responds to the mass and height of the other office buildings along the busy street. Its placement and form mediate between that context and the town hall behind it, which picks up on the scale of the nearby church. It is classically an atrium building with a square in front of it. The housing even deeper in the site, set in a soft landscape, is larger than that around it but smaller than the other buildings in the centre. Each building has a different material palette, which is characteristically reduced. But within this reduction are hidden considerable riches. The floor plans of the community hall, for instance, have four corridors, each of which forms an informal meeting place and is extended visually through a large window. But because the floors are rotated, the view in each direction is in a different place on each floor, which is just noticeable on the fully glazed exterior. These subtleties require a sophisticated structural system, which also frees up the exterior skin to be as delicate as it wishes.

The physical complexities of our contemporary cities and Morger & Degelo Architekten's matter-of-fact response and stringent vocabulary can again be seen in their St. Alban-Ring housing project in Basel. To one side of the narrow site are a motorway ramp and a railway line. On the other is a park with large school buildings within a neighbourhood of early-twentieth-century villas very near the city centre. The architects create a long building against the traffic and its noise, the form on the park side zigzagging monumentally, with continuous balconies to afford views to all. They then transform this into a gentle undulation on the street side that refers to the movement it faces and also breaks up the 120-metre-long façade. The stairwells are a loud red, which again breaks up the whiteness and the horizontality of the form. The plans adopt this two-sided character. There is only one place both sides can be seen at the same time, a core of private, nineteenth-century spaces appearing within a twentieth-century one.

Reinach town centre, Basel
[left] The town hall.
[below] The office block and town hall form a plaza on the street.
[opposite, top left] The space between the two housing blocks.
[opposite, top right] Site plan.
[opposite, below] A classic atrium for the town hall.

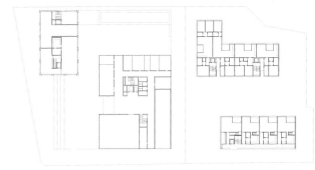

The singular House Müller again shows Morger & Degelo accepting what exists but then critiquing it by reflecting it. The area is a now-typical postwar suburban development of single-family houses, which sit in the middle of small plots. The client, however, wanted maximum privacy without even the trappings of bourgeois neighbourliness. Square in plan, the house's height makes it half a cube. It is almost completely closed. From the outside it is difficult to discern where the floors are, much less what is going on inside, so the design thwarts the harmless voyeurism that traditionally comes from walking by. Aside from a small core, the house is a single flowing space on each level. On the ground floor extensive glazing defines a courtyard and wraps inside to carve out a semi-enclosed space. Along with reflections from the outdoor water basin, it brings a mediated version of the outside in. On the top floor the bedroom is lit only from an interior courtyard, again carved out of the cube. The house uncompromisingly rejects its immediate neighbours, but has views of the church and the castle on opposite hills by virtue of two precisely placed windows. The exterior is hard and rather unforgiving, of grey in situ concrete, while the interior is much warmer though still not soft, much like the museum.

Valerio Olgiati

Schoolhouse, Paspels,
Graubünden
[pp.202–03] The setting
among the fields.
[below] The entrance
façade hints at the
rotation of the plan.

[opposite] The hillside
slides by the monolithic
building.

Coming from an architectural culture that is committed first and foremost to building, Valerio Olgiati describes a working method to which few in Switzerland would ascribe: 'we talk and discuss more than we draw'. The probing discussions and the development of the ideas that emerge from them result in buildings that are knowingly provocative, sometimes seriously mischievous. Each project begins with the examination of its simplest notions and of the acknowledged rules. Through the development of the design, however, the constraints can be challenged by manipulating slightly what is first accepted at face value.

Once the givens of a project have been subjected to this coolly challenging, almost didactic method, a building emerges. This can be clearly seen in Olgiati's scheme for an office building in Zurich. He is convinced that he won the investor-backed competition because his proposal provided the largest possible area. The form follows precisely the planning guidelines in relation to the adjacent sites as well as the regulation that upper storeys must step back. The consensus about where to place the core is accepted, though it is pulled apart. But such matter-of-factness allows for formal and even sculptural development. If the vertical structure is continuous from the top to the bottom floor, the columns must lean inwards and become closer together, but also carry a smaller and smaller floor plate. The columns and the floors can both

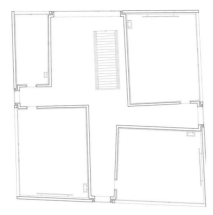

Schoolhouse,
Paspels, Graubünden
[p.206] Approach from
the street.

[p.207] The cruciform
interior corridor.
[left] Top-floor plan.

Schoolhouse,
Paspels, Graubünden
[opposite, below] Stair-
case and first floor.

[below] Top floor with
sloping ceiling and window
at the end of the corridor.

become thinner with increasing height above the ground. Such a way of working seeks to make aesthetic and even programmatic issues secondary. It is a relaxed or perhaps contrary attitude towards style and language. Just how provocative or even irritating the result can be is seen in a project of Olgiati's in Flims, where supermarkets, hiking shops and ski shops sprawl along one of the main roads to the mountains and their resorts. In the middle of the town, on a curve in the road, from where it can be seen from both directions, stands the glaringly white and abstract Yellow House.

The long-vacant building and a collection of local cultural artefacts were bequeathed to Flims by the important regional architect Rudolf Olgiati just before his death in 1995. He stipulated criteria for its renovation, namely, that it was to be a public building, had to be painted white from top to bottom and must have a stone roof. His son, Valerio Olgiati, was given the commission in 1997 to renovate and create a small museum for Flims. A radical approach was necessary, however, to make an old house suitable for exhibitions. Olgiati stripped out the interior, leaving a shell into which he set three identical timber floor structures that divide the space. In order to open up the interior he inserted a single, massive wooden column on each floor, at which the exposed crossbeams join. The column is the major space-forming element and is not placed in the centre. On the top floor it leans over to

Yellow House,
Flims, Graubünden
[opposite] The building's
position at the bend
in the road.
[below] The street façade
with entry stair to the right.

support the pyramidal roof in its centre, having mutated from a purely tectonic and spatial element below to a sculptural one above. Attention is drawn to the subtleties in the character of the space by painting everything white by way of a denial of materiality and an overstated acceptance of museum interiors. This also means that the interior quickly begins to look a bit worn from the visitors and even slightly battered since different materials move and deteriorate at different rates. And with the windows set flush to the interior one does feel the thinness and fragility of the interior surface, which is especially marked in contrast to the mass and texture of the outside.

The exterior received the most decisive and obvious manipulation. All shutters, balconies and accoutrements were removed. The smooth plaster characteristic of such houses was chipped away to reveal the rough rubble construction. The new openings, however, were formed with poured concrete and contrast with the texture of the exterior wall, as do the original openings that were filled in. Windows were set as deeply as possible towards the interior of the wall, which helps give the building an almost ghostly appearance. In order to create a single form, the original roof with its eaves is replaced with a roof pulled back to sit within the exterior walls; its stone shingles also painted white. This image of a spectre is reinforced by maintaining the name by which the house had long

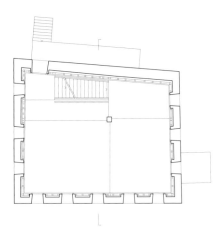

Yellow House
Flims, Graubünden
[opposite, top left]
Texture of the exterior
wall in contrast to the
window surround.
[opposite, top right] The
ghostly effect of the deep-
set windows.
[opposite, below] The
abstraction achieved by
having everything white.
[left] Floor plan.
[below] Column leaning
over to the centre of
the roof.

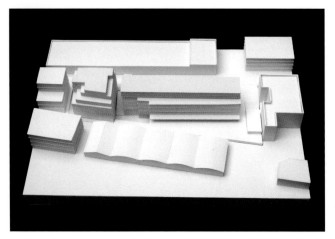

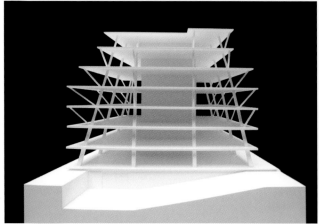

been known. In the end it is difficult to know quite what is old and what is new, though the building has obviously been made more abstract. Olgiati likens his approach here to Beuys's paintings of a live animal, in which the subject was almost embarrassed by itself. The town plays an important part in the tourist infrastructure of Graubünden but is itself rather uncharming. The Yellow House's monumentality stands in contrast to the holiday village, its traffic jams and picturesque chalets.

Just how varied the results can be from Olgiati's approach is seen in a school building he designed in the mountains. The village of Paspels is really a scattered settlement of free-standing buildings set among fields, and the architect adopts this figure ground. The school is indeed the monolith the locals have dubbed it. It is built of massive concrete, the form is based on a square, the roof follows the slope of the hill, there is no forecourt before the entrance, some of the windows are flush with the exterior and the bronze doors and roof over the entrance are monumental. It stoutly ignores the charming, low-rise 1950s school building across from it, to which it is connected underground. But, typically for a building by Olgiati, things do not mean what they first seem. The slight distortions in the form, the urbanity of the bronze windows and the shifting of the openings all give it a slightly uncertain character and hint at the forces within.

Three different-sized classrooms and a storage room are situated in the corners. Each room is of different proportions and opens to the landscape in a different direction. To ensure the individuality of each room further the second floor is rotated 90 degrees and follows the form of the roof. The corridor is the empty space between the rooms, broadening out near the stair and the regular light of the northeast. But the generous size of the circulation space and the window at the end of each arm give an interesting equality between the space and the classrooms. While the diagram is Palladian, the space inside is anything but static. Each room has a kind of foyer where the irregular geometry is most perceptible because the classroom walls themselves are square but perpendicular to only one of the exterior walls. While designing it Olgiati had experimented by twisting the form slightly. The effect was powerful, making the space inside dynamic. Because he wanted this to be felt more than simply seen, he had his office work up numerous models to see how little one needed to distort the form out of square for it to be just noticeable. They learned that if the distortion was less than five degrees it was not perceptible, and accordingly this was the degree of twisting that was put into effect.

The exterior contrast between the massive, single-pour concrete and the bronze windows is played out again in the interior. The classroom floors, walls and ceiling are

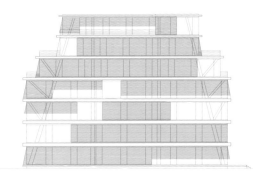

Office building, Zurich
[opposite, left] Site model.
[opposite, right] Structural model.
[left] Façade.

lined with larch and are warm and cosy. The two spaces contrast strongly in terms of acoustics, light and climate. The classroom windows sit towards the interior of the wall and span its entire length, bringing the landscape into the classroom like a picture, while in the corridors the windows are flush with the exterior to emphasize its mass from the inside. The building's departure from orthogonality is only just perceptible on the interior; on the exterior it creates a slight disturbance.

Unlike most of his peers, Olgiati is not pursuing a classic *recherche architecturale* but with his work is holding up a distorting mirror to the culture of which he is also a part.

Peter Zumthor

Sound Box, Hanover Expo
2000, Germany
[pp. 216–17] Exterior of
the Swiss pavilion or
Sound Box.

[below] Within the Expo
context.
[opposite] The feel of
a labyrinth.

Architects can achieve a status close to fame, and their buildings, or images of them, almost iconic status far beyond the profession. Complicit in this culture of celebrity is a prolific international industry of magazines and books that can even provide the fame without the building. But this media-friendly model of the architect can favour or perhaps even inspire a highly polished architecture that puts other considerations ahead of fundamental concerns such as place and the poetry of construction. It sometimes seems as if the world of architecture divides into the heady, opportunistic camp that embraces shopping, fashion and travel and the conservative camp that complains that current architecture is superficial, pedantic and in thrall to neo-avant-gardists. Peter Zumthor stubbornly avoids setting foot in either camp, while clearly being one of the finest architects in the world today.

Peter Zumthor is probably best known for the thermal baths in Vals, a building extraordinary in its connection to its valley and community, the rigour of its plan, the innovation of its construction, the precision of its materials and the sensuality of the experience. The baths are a good example of many of the qualities of his work, the most important of which is the primacy of the architectural experience. This may sound tautological, but Zumthor's buildings insist on reminding us of those elemental architectural qualities that we are sometimes in too much of a

rush to appreciate or think ourselves too sophisticated to remember. And it is precisely with recollections that he begins every project: 'In my mind, I envisage what it will feel like to live in the house I am designing, I try to imagine its physical emanations, recalling at the same time all the experiences of place and space we are capable of making, those that we have made and those that we have yet to make, and I dream of the experiences I would like us to make in the house as yet unbuilt.' (Peter Zumthor, *Peter Zumthor Works*, 1998, p.7)

Zumthor's ability to recall the fundamental elements of architecture and make them manifest again means that he can work at any scale, with any material, seemingly with any programme, and ignore the question of style. His buildings, each of which is noteworthy, range from the almost furniture-like wooden chapel at Sogn Benedetg to the cool and ambiguous scale of the Kunsthaus Bregenz, from the horror-laden centre for the documentation of Nazi terror to the luminosity of Kolumba Diocesan Museum in Cologne. Common to all these diverse projects are precision and a poetic use of materials.

The primacy of experience can also be understood in opposition to didacticism, even when one is designing a building within which to exhibit documents relating to the Nazi period. The competition for Topography of Terror asked for an exhibition space and offices at what was

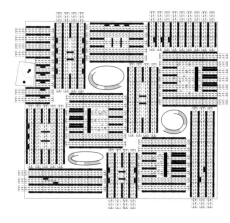

Sound Box, Hanover
Expo 2000, Germany
[p.220] A space where
words are projected onto
the wall.
[p.221, left] One of the
sound rooms.

[p.221, right] An elliptical
room carved out of the
pavilion's rectilinearity.
[opposite and below]
One of the cafés.
[left] The plan.

Topography of Terror,
Berlin, Germany
[left] The building as a
fence just demarcating
inside from outside.
[below] The entrance and
smaller building protecting
the ruins.
[opposite, top] First-floor
plan.
[opposite, below] Ground-
floor plan.

once Europe's most terrifying address, the administrative
centre of Nazi Germany's security services and police.
On seeing the site for the first time Zumthor was not
sure that he could design a building there. But his next
thought was that it was important to build something at
the place where those horrors either happened or were
managed. The actual site – the few vestiges of buildings
and mounds of rubble – led him to the idea of a building
like a fence, touching the ground lightly, enclosing it
more than containing it. It should not be brutal or dreary
but beautiful and meditative. It need not replicate or simu-
late its contents. Rather, it would provide an environment
where one could understand and experience the place
and its meaning.

The perimeter of the building consists of an outer wall
of piers, in the centre of which is a layer of frameless
single glazing. An inner layer creates spaces and enclo-
sures. This pure construction only moderates the interior
temperature. Although fully half of the surface is glazed,
to the viewer moving about it appears solid. From the
inside one is always drawn to the site visually through
the frame of the columns, which provide a connection
with the ground.

The idea that the place itself is almost sacred directs not
only the design of the building but that of the interior as
well. Zumthor has insisted that it be similarly elemental –

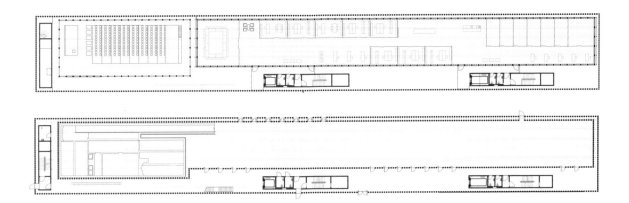

direct and connected to the place. Nothing is covered, plastered or concealed. The ground-floor exhibition will contain excavations and an area filled with rows of tables on which are placed genuine documents. Nothing should hang from the ceiling or be connected to the building. Everything should be connected to this historic ground, which is designed to be continuous with the ground outside.

Of course, the primacy of experience with a different programme can lead to a much lighter, more festive experience. In the bustle of the Hanover Expo 2000 Zumthor designed a Sound Box (*Klangkörper*) to be the Swiss national pavilion. In its form and construction it could hardly be simpler: wooden beams, with spacers between them, as when timber is stacked to dry. Steel tension rods and springs keep the walls stable as they naturally dry out and shrink. The scale, though, is astonishing, however one calculates it: 5,000 cubic metres of construction-grade spruce; 52 x 56 metres arranged as twelve stacks, each 9 metres tall; 40,000 wood beams.

The Sound Box is not, however, a minimalist sculpture but presents characteristics of Switzerland. It is emphatically not didactic. It makes no attempt to put forward either praise or self-criticism. The concept, rather, is Switzerland as a cultured host and thus an oasis for exhausted Expo visitors. The elemental, even rural architectural elements

combine with sound, word, drink, food and clothing to create a sensual, rich experience. It is, boldly, a total work of art (*Gesamtkunstwerk*).

Within this complete control, experiences are nevertheless consciously left to happen. The form is like a labyrinth. Twelve stacks of wood are set perpendicular to each other and the structure has over fifty entrances or exits. There are bars, stairways, small open spaces and sound spaces. The musical concept was commissioned from Daniel Ott and requires 350 musicians in total, or twelve in three-hour shifts. One hears music all the time, but it changes. Accordions and dulcimers produce a kind of acoustic background. Soloists are choreographed to change their spatial and musical position. At prescribed times they meet in certain spaces, only to disperse again. Some of the music is written, some is improvised in two-minute bursts. So the music is structured and varied according to the rooms and the time. The precision of the design and the almost overwhelming sensuality of it all contrast markedly with typical Expo architecture. The experience of the pavilion changes according to the number of visitors, the season, the wind and the weather, as the changing light is filtered through the timber screens, not to mention a visitor's own mood or preconceptions. This architecture explicitly rejects using mediated images in favour of working as a direct presence or experience.

Single-family house,
Graubünden
[below] The house's
cruciform diagram on
the exterior.
[opposite, top left] The
kitchen overlooks a valley.

[opposite, top right] One
of the many stairways.
[opposite, below] A bed-
room with its own balcony
and staircase.

Single-family house,
Graubünden
[opposite, top from left to
right] Ground-, first- and
second-floor plans.

[opposite, below] Timber
forms the structure and
surface of the interior, as
seen on the first floor.

In the case of the Kunsthaus in Bregenz, the architecture invites a direct experience of the art that is exhibited but also of the natural qualities of being on Lake Constance. The outer skin is assembled from finely etched glass panels hung like shingles. Being all the same size and visibly held in place by clamps, they give the form an ambiguous scale. From the exterior the building is likewise enigmatic, becoming different with the changing characteristics of light by the lake and glowing at night. Its translucency affords intimations of movement or inner life. The glass box takes its place among the row of buildings along the bay. All the other programmes that so often take precedence over the space for art – bar, book-shop, offices – are pulled out of the building and into their own black box. This two-storey building is positioned on the street side of the site to define a public space.

The clear separation of the lake and town side, translucency and opacity, the strict space of contemplation and the urbane one of socializing allow an architectural reduction of materiality, space and light. The space-defining elements of the interior can be monolithic because the extensive technical requirements of an exhibition space are cleverly integrated into the exterior envelope and the ceilings. They need not be built in layers and are not painted or clad. They have an immediate sensual presence. The floor and stairs are polished and hard, the walls and ceilings brittle and velvety. Daylight entering the tall space between

floors is diffused through the glass ceiling and so changes according to the time of day or changing weather. Superficially the interior resembles the now classic reduction of the gallery, but for all its reduction it is not neutral but highly sensuous and connected to the world.

Although Zumthor is world-famous and much in demand by clients, he has chosen to keep his practice small so as not to compromise the way he works, rather than allowing it to grow to match the demand for his services. Consequently, he turns down most commissions, accepting a project only when it has the potential to be a good building. Although that might seem to mean extraordinary programmes – thermal baths, a winery, a chapel – his decision actually hinges more on his sense of the potential for working with the client. A single-family house in Graubünden at first seems an unduly modest project for an architect of Zumthor's stature. The clients are a local family who wanted to build a house for themselves in their village and in the local tradition of massive timber. They also wanted to work on it themselves.

Zumthor works and lives in a village and could understand the clients and feel what they were after. Wishing to contribute something to the area where he lives, he agreed to design a simple, large, massive timber house for them. He didn't know exactly what it would be possible

Kunsthaus, Bregenz, Austria
[opposite] The semi-transparent façade is made from equally sized glass shingles.

[below] The black opaque café and the translucent gallery box form two sides of the courtyard.

Kunsthaus, Bregenz,
Austria
[below] Ground floor.

[opposite] Staircase
leading up to the galleries.

to do, but he could recall the fantastic feeling of being in such houses. Massive timber building is an old-fashioned technique with certain limitations. Structurally it is difficult to have large openings; the plan tends towards a square; and the exposed crossing of the walls at the corners allows rain to weaken them. Characteristically, Zumthor found a way to work with this technique and yet to create something new.

The clients have six children and wanted a house with four bedrooms. The basic organization consists of five towers, four at the corners and one in the centre, which act as structural entities. Between these towers are the actual living spaces, which can have huge openings. It is a Palladian diagram. The tower in the centre contains the bathroom and toilets, each corner containing vertical means of circulation. The result is a house that is tradi-tional and yet abstract. The five towers are barely visible in the façades. The walls and floors read as planes. The uninsulated roof, a traditional place to hang meats, is extremely thin and sits delicately on the frame below.

The result spatially is that every bedroom upstairs is reached through its own stairway and has its own balcony. The only communal space on the bedroom level is the large central bathroom. On the ground floor the spaces revolve around the centre and flow into each other. From any of these rooms one can see into another room and

Kunsthaus, Bregenz, Austria

[left] The structural concrete walls, behind which sits the vertical circulation.

[below] Gallery interior. Ground-floor plan [opposite, left] and upper-level plan [opposite, right].

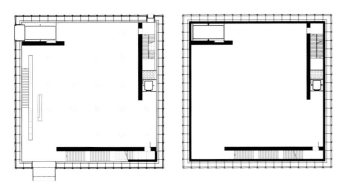

through the house to the outside. They thus work in the opposite manner to the bedroom level, which is composed of discrete spaces that meet in the centre. There are no corridors on either of the two main floors. The entrance to the house is unfussy. One enters a vestibule off which leads a guest apartment or a dark corridor with a stair around the corner. This area gives little clue to the degree of organizational eccentricity in the overall design.

The construction is clever and typically precise. The four corners containing circulation consist of two layers with a cavity in between for insulation. This allows all the interior walls to be single-thickness. They are left raw. The larch floors are oiled. The inhabitant of the house is thus completely contained in wood. Services run horizontally under the built-up floors or vertically through holes drilled through the solid timber. Massive timber compresses over time as it dries. The terrazzo slabs for the bathrooms, with the aggregate chosen by the clients from a brook in Davos, are hung from the walls so that they can move with them. Likewise, the wooden stairs are connected to the walls in such a way as to allow them to move as the house dries. The problem of rot at the exterior crossing corners is resolved by having only one wall protrude. The other is dove-tailed into it, much as in furniture.

The house belongs very much to its valley, to the clients and to its type of construction. The clients felled the wood locally and stored it for eight years to age. They chose trees from the same side of the valley as the site, its north side. The exterior is allowed to weather according to its orientation. As in traditional timber buildings, it will become black on the sunny side and grey on the shadier sides.

What makes Zumthor's work so special is not just the care and the control he exercises in every project. Rather it is his insistence on the continuing power of elemental architectural qualities. In this way he may seem old-fashioned, but the work itself is very much of its place and time. As he himself says, 'the thought process is not abstract but works with spatial images. It has sensuous components. It uses the images of places and spaces to which we have access, which we remember. In other words: thought travels through a specific space which contains traces of place and architecture.' (loc. cit.)

Essentially Realism

On the importance of construction in contemporary architecture in German-speaking Switzerland

Martin Tschanz

'Although a certain dryness is apparent, the ... superb quality of construction set the highest standards.' Nearly every comment on modern Swiss architecture echoes G. E. Kidder-Smith's observation in his 1950 book *Switzerland Builds*.[1] The theme of construction seems to be virtually unavoidable, although opinions vary from admiration for the extraordinary thoroughness of the Swiss to criticism of their excessive love of detail.

This fits in perfectly with the whole canon of Swiss national characteristics,[2] which incorporates the cliché of the land of herdsmen, cheese and chocolate, as well as of the clock-maker, the precision engineer and the pernickety fiddler. It includes a focus on quality and a Protestant work ethic, as well as a predilection for particularly elegant but always functional solutions to problems of whatever kind.

Embodying this whole theme – if one may be forgiven for mentioning this rather tired old icon – is the Swiss army knife. First and foremost it is a sophisticated, practical tool. But it is also – and this is what distinguishes it fundamentally from most such multifunctional tools – a real joy to handle; it is a true representative of 'beauty as function',[3] conveying all sorts of meanings and associations, whether in the Swiss-red version for officers and tourists or in the less conspicuous but handier version used by ordinary soldiers.

Architecture in the polytechnic tradition

At least since the foundation in 1855 of the Eidgenössische Technische Hochschule (ETH, Swiss Federal Institute of Technology), Swiss architects have been trained essentially in a polytechnic tradition. The art-oriented culture of the academies has had little or no part to play, and even the modern, swiftly expanding Accademia di Architettura in Mendrisio [4] has generally followed the same line, being more devoted to the polytechnic tradition than its name might imply.

Consequently, at the centre of architectonic thought lies construction, in all its physical, material and economic manifestations. The structural, constructive execution of a project is generally seen as integral to the whole process of design, which itself is regarded as a matter of pin-pointing and solving problems that are of a more or less concrete nature.

Against such a background, it is scarcely surprising that there is a highly developed culture of cooperation between engineers and architects, which goes beyond the traditional tasks of the architect–engineer. Such outstanding engineers as Robert Maillart, Heinz Hossdorf and Jürg Conzett found and still find interested and capable partners among their architect colleagues, and vice versa. A building such as the Volta Schoolhouse in Basel, to take just one example, could be conceived only through the common interests and language of designers and engineers and the willingness and ability of both sides to tackle the structural and spatial problems together.

The architect's desire to control construction, much as an artist controls brush and paint, is reflected in the structure of the profession. Small to medium-sized firms, often with fewer than a dozen staff, dominate the Swiss architectural landscape. As far as possible they all try to eliminate the gap between design and execution. The architect still sees himself as an all-rounder, in charge of the project from initial concept to final execution. Even today it is not unusual for the architect to oversee construction and for individual subcontractors and craftsmen to be directly under his supervision. Indeed, until recently this was fairly standard practice.

Current trends towards specialization and globalization, however, have put pressure on this view of the profession, even in Switzerland, and there is no doubt that profound changes are now taking place. It must be said, though, that there is a good deal more stability and capacity for development than some people had initially expected from these changes. For instance, the open market introduced by GATT and WTO was thought to be the end of the established form of architectural competition, because the customary regional procedural restrictions were no longer possible. Today, however, there seems to be a contrary trend, for in the innumerable architectural competitions it is the newer, smaller firms that, time and again, come out on top. Here Swiss federalism and the concomitant smallness of the bodies that take decisions on public commissions probably play an important part. For instance, the school system in Switzerland is organized primarily by local communities. Most of the 2,800-plus local councils plan and build their schools independently, and particularly in rural areas these are often the most important public buildings. Even today some of them are commissioned through open competitions. When the process is restricted, as is more frequently the case – e.g. after preliminary rounds – it is common practice for invitations to go out to a mixture of new and established, local and national firms. Close links between political decision-makers, clients, builders and consumers are beneficial in projects that provide concrete, rational solutions to specific needs and circumstances. What is merely fashionable or spectacular is not so likely to obtain official blessing under such conditions.

In Switzerland the highly developed culture of cooperation would seem to be a particularly important key to the future. Since the 1930s there have been widespread, more or less solid mergers between architects, and nowadays lone wolves are rare exceptions in the profession. A common background, derived from training at ETH in Zurich or at a comparable university, and the whole culture of a problem-oriented vocation create a good basis for cooperatives, reaching far beyond the borders of individual disciplines. Increasingly, particular projects

bring about link-ups between independent firms, and in this way they not only fill their respective gaps but also exchange ideas. Thus the smaller, slimmer companies can become at least potentially competitive even when faced with more complex projects.

Tectonics, essentialism and structuralism

In the history of modern German–Swiss architecture, one can always detect a strong affinity, despite various changes, to the architecture of the 1940s and 1950s – an affinity that is connected, even if not exclusively, with the construction culture of the time. Especially in the 1980s, among all the postmodern excesses, one could see in this earlier, so-called new art of building [5] certain evolutionary starting-points. In the 1940s, materials and constructions were handled with a sometimes almost playful virtuosity in the quest for such long-lost qualities as sensuousness and sensuality, differentiation of scale and ornamentation – though without ever losing sight of the modern demand for functionality. In the mid-1980s, there were countless examples of a similar culture of tectonics, for instance in the early buildings of Herzog & de Meuron, Burkhalter Sumi Architekten, Peter Zumthor and others: here we find a delicate form of architecture, full of details, beautiful profiles and expressive nodes in which the poetry arises essentially from a carefully articulated language of construction.

By then, however, technical and economic conditions had undergone a drastic change. Building regulations now demanded efficient insulation, and in practical terms this meant virtually wrapping up the whole edifice, unless it happened to be made of wood. Indeed, if an architectural language was to give direct expression to the architectural requirements while keeping the budget within manageable proportions, wood was the only material that *could* be used.

Swiss officer's knife, Victorinox.

Miller & Maranta, Volta Schoolhouse, Basel, 1996–2000.

Herzog & de Meuron, factory and warehouse for Ricola, Mülhausen, France, 1991–93.

Peter Zumthor, Kunsthaus, Bregenz, Austria, 1990–97.

Morger & Degelo Architekten and Christian Kerez, Art Museum, Vaduz, Liechtenstein, 1998–2000.

Von Ballmoos Krucker Architekten, e-science lab (study), ETH, Zurich, 2002.

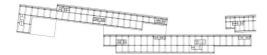

Marcel Meili, Markus Peter Architekten,
Albtal by Ettlingen, 1990.

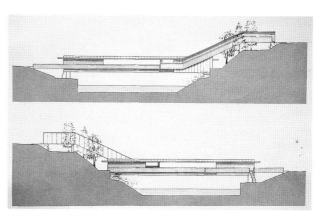

Marcel Meili, Markus Peter Architekten,
Branger & Conzett Engineers, Mursteg Bridge,
Murau, Austria, 1995.

Herzog & de Meuron, apartments
at a firewall, Basel, 1987–88.

Peter Zumthor, Thermal bath,
Vals, Graubünden, 1990–96.

Cover of *archithese*, 2/1980,
issue devoted to architects
Häfeli, Moser & Steiger.

Marcel Meili, Markus Peter Architekten,
roof of railway station, Zurich, 1997.

An alternative, however, which was developed for many projects was the tectonic wrapping of buildings, the coverings themselves becoming a focus of attention. Examples of this are Diener & Diener's office block in Picassoplatz, Basel, where the image of brackets and hanging slabs is legible, or Gigon & Guyer's Kirchner Museum in Davos, with its glass and insulation cover clapped on top of its concrete heart. A high point and perhaps even an end point in this development is undoubtedly Peter Zumthor's Kunsthaus in Bregenz, where the tension between body and skin has been carried to its logical extreme and has become the driving force of the whole architectural concept.

In many cases nowadays, though, there is no constructional articulation and instead attention is drawn to the covered body and the impact of surfaces and materials. New effects are tested. Familiar materials are taken from their normal contexts and can thus be experienced in new ways, while new techniques can also be applied to old materials. Roofing felt, scobalit (a translucent fibreglass panel) and other 'low-class' substances can be ennobled by unusual applications, concrete can be coloured, textured or processed, the joints compressed, glass can be etched or printed. Since the main focus is on the effects of materials and forms, every effort is made to shut out anything that distracts attention from it. Often it entails a considerable increase in cost as well as much architectural expertise to keep the construction hidden from view.

This approach might be termed 'essentialism': it should be possible to experience the effects directly and in their purest form. An apt analogy in this context is minimal art, and in particular the boxlike 'specific objects' of Donald Judd – who refused to call them sculptures – and the works of Tony Smith.[6] Indeed, some of these buildings are more like intriguing groups of sculptures than houses. This proximity to art is certainly not without its problems. Sometimes elementary architectonic functions can barely be fulfilled, such as the connection between interior and exterior. Furthermore, such objects 'this side of signs'[7] tend to be culturally hermetic, concentrating autistically on themselves and shutting themselves off from any meaningful reference to the outside world.

The Kunstmuseum in Vaduz, by the architects Morger & Degelo Architekten and Christian Kerez, would seem with its rigorous radicalism to mark a climax to this essentialist development. The monolithic concrete, seemingly cast without any joints, together with its black and coloured appendages, has been smoothed and polished to such powerful effect that its structural appearance is one of pure surface: shining, reflecting and without any depth.[8] Instead of the proverbial black box that is open to all eventualities, this reminds one of the black monolith that plays a central role in Stanley Kubrick's *Space Odyssey 2001* – the hermetic object *par excellence*.

In recent years, however, there have been increasing signs of structuralist approaches in various Swiss building projects. An example is Thomas von Ballmoos and Bruno Krucker's entry in the competition for the new IT building at ETH Zurich, and it is no coincidence that Krucker and other architects are currently very interested in the work of Alison and Peter Smithson.[9]

This development is unquestionably most strikingly typified by the works of Marcel Meili, Markus Peter Architekten, in which there are evident signs of a 'patient research' into the architectonic dimension of structure. These architects are reacting not least against the immensely demanding conditions of current building programmes; they are not committed to a markedly fast-moving genre of architecture, but are at pains to work on the surviving permanent elements of development and construction and to make these architecturally effective. This concept is essentially familiar to the structuralism and metabolism of the 1960s, but it heads in a different direction. Meili and Peter's constructions are not confined to dynamic organization and articulation, but create spaces, define forms and are precisely geared to urban development.

This, then, is a structuralism that integrates all the experiences of recent architecture with urban space, typology, form and the aesthetics of effect. Examples of their approach are their urban development studies for the Albtal near Esslingen (1990)[10] and the Richti-Areal in Zurich Wallisellen (together with M.-C. Bétrix and E. Consolascio, 1991)[11]. The same approach, however, is to be found in the little bridge in Murau (with Jürg Conzett). This is certainly architecture of great formal density with marked sculptural qualities. And it is the structure itself that is spatially active here, joining and dividing the paths and establishing its links with town and countryside.

A means or an end in itself?

In 1994 Hans Frei wrote an article in the magazine *archithese* sharply criticizing modern German–Swiss architecture at precisely the time when it had begun to gain a high degree of international recognition. Under the polemic title 'Museum für sauber gelöste Details' (Museum for Neatly Kept Details),[12] he launched a particularly scathing attack on the general spread of perfectionism: 'Such thinking does not just begin with detail, it ends with it too.' He was prepared to exclude only 'the best buildings' from this attack, for these did not allow themselves to follow 'the general direction of the German-Swiss tendency'.[13] It may be said, however, that his view of this 'general direction' was rather too restricted, and his critique, albeit extremely stimulating, lays itself open to the same charge of over-simplification as he levelled against Swiss architecture. For the latter is, fortunately, often richer than the discourse that describes it, and indeed its very essence seems to involve complexity and – in successful examples – the integration of diverse factors into a unified whole.

This categorization of constructive principles also needs to be qualified: on the one hand, they are rarely to be found in any pure form, and on the other they are clearly not enough on their own to explain the type of architecture in question. In Herzog & de Meuron's early house in a Basel courtyard, for instance, the principle of tectonics is not just meant to heighten the artistic effect of the construction, but goes much further: the exceptionally careful design of this wooden structure is very precisely geared to its concrete situation in an urban courtyard. It creates an intriguing contrast with the wall that supports the house, and enters into a sort of dialogue with other, simpler wooden structures in the neighbourhood.

Similarly, the stone world of Zumthor's thermal baths in Vals certainly makes a direct impact through its sensuousness, but the structure of bodies and slabs can also be read tectonically, as can the wide range of associations and levels of meaning that these contain.[14]

The unusual proportions of the platform roofs at Zurich railway station (M. Meili and M. Peter with Axel Fickert and Kaschica Knapkiewicz) are not just an end in themselves, but make a precise statement about urban development, articulating a clear attitude towards what constitutes the essence of a modern station.

In all these examples, the construction is more than a mere means to an end, but it is still only part of an architecture that can just as well be approached from the standpoint of programme, location or form.

In this context, experiments with unusual materials and techniques – even allowing for certain undeniable mannerisms – should be seen above all as attempts to extend the architectonic palette. Nowadays there are – fortunately – fewer laurels awarded merely for the charm of novelty. It is therefore no surprise that there has been a return to simpler, more conventional methods, particularly among younger architects. Plastering as a form of exterior insulation, long despised, has been back in favour for quite some time, and there are innumerable projects that are now making full use of the particular qualities of plaster and paint.

Realism

In discussing the constructional culture of Swiss architecture, one might also talk of realism. This term has been a constant architectural thread in Switzerland since the 1970s [15] and perhaps owes its longevity to the fact that it cannot be pinned to any precise definition. Nevertheless, it seems to encompass an essential element of Swiss architecture – its basis in solid, everyday reality, which it both interprets [16] and transmutes into characteristic forms of art. This is an architecture that starts out from the polytechnic culture of problem-solving and creates works that point to something beyond pure functionality and specific cases. A part of this culture is the obligation to build the 'difficult whole,' which embraces complexity and integrates a variety of conditions and influences, while at the same time allowing only those contradictions that will not jeopardize the unity of the work. [17] In other words, we have here a synthesis in which construction is one important aspect, but only one – just as functionality is only one aspect of the Swiss army knife.

To focus exclusively on constructional details will therefore lead the observer to false conclusions. For instance, the sophisticated, multilayered glaze in shades of mother-of-pearl that Miller & Maranta used on their Volta school building in Basel may in isolation seem mannered and exaggerated. In its actual setting, however, it is entirely appropriate. The care and attention lavished on this feature were entirely necessary, because the extreme depth of the building meant that light in the inner courtyards and spaces was at a premium owing to the choice of typology and structure; all of this is inextricably linked to the specific site and to the history of the location, as well as to a particular concept of the school as an institution. Special treatment of the inner courtyards was therefore an integral part of the architectural planning right from the start, even if the chosen solution developed only gradually as the project proceeded.

Nevertheless, the reality of such a detail is something that can, of course, never be taken for granted. It all depends on the existence of an architectural culture, which is – still? – present in Switzerland and in which architects continue to devote their talents and their enthusiasm to the pursuit of appropriate research and, perhaps for this very reason, earn the respect of the investors who are their partners. This culture also embraces the clients and the political decision-makers, who must be both willing and able to engage in such projects and to have confidence in the architects concerned.

Notes

[1] G. E. Kidder-Smith, *Switzerland Builds*, New York, 1950, p. 83.

[2] For more detail on the 'Swissness' of Swiss architecture, see Werner Oechslin, 'Helvetia docet', in *Architektur im 20. Jahrhundert: Schweiz*, Munich, Prestel, 1998, pp. 55–60.

[3] Max Bill, 'Schönheit auf Funktion und als Funktion', in *Werk*, 1949, pp. 272–74.

[4] See www.arch.unisi.ch.

[5] 'Der Entwicklung der Architektur in den Jahren vor dem Kriege und in den Kriegsjahren könnte man den Titel geben, "Vom Neuen Bauen zur Neuen Baukunst".' ['To the development of architecture in the years before the war and during the war one might apply the designation "from new building to new architecture"']: Hans Hoffmann, typescript, in Christoph Luchsinger, *Hans Hoffmann*, Zurich, 1985, p. 136. The translation published in the exhibition catalogue for *Switzerland – Planning and Building* (London,1946), speaks rather less pithily of a 'transition from the science of building to the art of building' (p. 20).

[6] See for example Martin Steinmann, 'The Presence of Things' in *Construction, Intention, Detail: Five Projects from Five Swiss Architects/Fünf Projekte von fünf Schweizer Architekten*, exhibition catalogue. Zurich, Artemis, 1994 (2nd ed.), pp. 8–25; Hans Frei, 'Stützen und Lasten: ein Parabel', in *archithese*, 5/1996, pp. 9–17.

[7] Martin Steinmann, 'La forme forte – En deçà des

signes', in *Faces*, no. 19, 1991, pp. 4–13 (German text in supplement pp. 1–4).

[8] See Hans Frei, 'Gesichtslose Haut', *Werk, Bauen & Wohnen*, no. 3/2001, pp. 26–33.

[9] *Peter Smithson*, Zurich, GTA, 2002; Thomas Schregenberger, '"As Found" – Ein aktueller Blick auf den Brutalismus', in *archithese*, 2/1997, pp. 42–45; Claude Lichtenstein (ed.), 'As Found – Die Entdeckung des Gewöhnlichen', exhibition catalogue, Zurich, 2001.

[10] *Werk, Bauen & Wohnen*, no. 11/1991, pp. 24–35.

[11] *Werk, Bauen & Wohnen*, no. 7, 8/1991, pp. 36–41.

[12] Hans Frei, 'Museum für sauber gelöste Details – Zur neuen Deutschschweizer Architektur', in *archithese*, 2/1994, pp. 68–71.

[13] Ibid, p. 70.

[14] See Peter Zumthor, Martin Tschanz, 'Das spezifische Gewicht der Architektur', in *archithese*, 5/1996, pp. 28–35, and Akos Moravanszky, 'Die sich selbst erzählende Welt – Peter Zumthor's Thermalbad in Vals und die Phänomenologie des Sehens', in *Architektur im 20. Jahrhundert: Schweiz*, Munich, Prestel, 1998.

[15] *archithese*, 19/1976, special issue on 'Realismus', guest editors Bruno Reichlin and Martin Steinmann.

[16] See Martin Tschanz, 'Entwurf als Interpretation?', in *archithese*, 2/1997, pp. 11–17.

[17] Closely akin to but also distinguishable from Robert Venturi. See Robert Venturi, *Complexity and Contradiction in Architecture*, New York, Museum of Modern Art, 1966.

Architect biographies

__Bearth + Deplazes__ Valentin Bearth graduated from ETH Zurich in 1983. Between 1984 and 1988 he worked in the office of Peter Zumthor in Haldenstein. In 1988 he set up his own practice in partnership with Andrea Deplazes. Since 2000 Bearth has been visiting professor at the Accademia di architettura in Mendrisio. Andrea Deplazes graduated from ETH Zurich in 1988. Since then he has been in partnership with Valentin Bearth. He has been professor of architecture and construction at ETH Zurich since 1997.

__Burkhalter Sumi Architekten__ Marianne Burkhalter trained as a technical draughtsman in the office of Hubacher and Issler in Zurich. In the 1970s she spent several years working and studying with Superstudio in Florence and with Studio Works in New York City and Los Angeles. She had two spells working as an assistant at ETH Zurich. Since 1984 she has shared a practice with Christian Sumi and has been a visiting professor at SCI-Arc in Los Angeles and in Ticino, and at EPF Lausanne. She is a member of the Commission on the Cityscape, Zurich. Christian Sumi gained a diploma at ETH Zurich, afterwards working at the German Archaeological Institute in Rome (DAI). He was a research fellow at the Institute for History and Theory of Architecture, working on Le Corbusier and the Immeuble Clarté in Geneva. From 1985 to 1987 he was assistant to Professor Bruno Reichlin at the School of Architecture, University of Geneva, and from 1989 to 1991 diploma adviser to Professor Mario Campi at ETH Zurich. He has been visiting professor at the School of Architecture, University of Geneva, the Graduate School of Design (GSD) at Harvard University, Cambridge, USA, at SCI-Arc in Ticino and at EPF Lausanne. Burkhalter and Sumi have exhibited and lectured widely.

After an apprenticeship as a carpenter __Gion A. Caminada__ studied at the School of Applied Arts in Zurich and then at ETH Zurich. After obtaining his degree in architecture he opened his own practice in Vrin. Since 1998 he has been an assistant professor at ETH Zurich.

__Jürg Conzett__ worked for six years in Peter Zumthor's office after gaining his diploma as a construction engineer. He opened a practice on his own in 1988, to be joined in 1992 by A. Branger. Since 1985 he has been a lecturer and since 1998 director of timber construction at the HTL in Chur. In 1999 he went into practice in Chur with Gianfranco Bronzini, a lecturer in construction at the HTW (Hochschule für Technik und Wirtschaft) since 1994, and Patrick Gartmann, who was assistant to Valerio Olgiati at ETH Zurich 1998–2000.

__Diener & Diener__ The firm was founded in 1942 by Marcus Diener. His son Roger joined in 1976, becoming a partner in 1980. Other partners in the firm are Dieter Righetti and Andreas Rüedi. They have been the subject of many exhibitions and are increasingly active across Europe. Diener was born in Basel in 1950 and graduated from ETH Zurich in 1975. He has been a visiting professor at EPF Lausanne, Harvard's GSD, Vienna, Amsterdam and Copenhagen. Since 1999 he has been professor at the Studio Basel of ETH Zurich with Jacques Herzog, Marcel Meili and Pierre de Meuron.

__Gigon & Guyer__ Annette Gigon and Mike Guyer founded their practice in 1989. Gigon, born in 1959, gained her diploma from ETH Zurich in 1984 and worked with Marbach & Rüegg in Zurich and Herzog & de Meuron in Basel before setting up her own office in 1987. Guyer, born in 1958, gained his diploma in 1984 from ETH Zurich and worked with OMA in Rotterdam and as an assistant to Professor Hans Kollhoff at ETH Zurich before setting up his own office in 1987. Gigon and Guyer have lectured widely and in 2001 were visiting professors at EPF Lausanne.

Marcel Meili, Markus Peter Architekten Markus Peter graduated from the HTL in Winterthur. Between 1985 and 1986 he collaborated with the practice of Professor Dolf Schnebli. From 1986 to 1988 he was assistant to Professor Mario Campi at ETH. In 1987 he started to work in partnership with Marcel Meili. After having been visiting lecturer 1993–95, Peter became professor for architecture and construction at ETH Zurich in 2002. Marcel Meili graduated from ETH in Zurich in 1980. From 1980 to 1982 he worked in the practice of Professor Dolf Schnebli. Between 1985 and 1987 he was research assistant to Professor Mario Campi. Since 1988 he has taught at different schools, such as the School of Applied Arts in Zurich, the GSD at Harvard and ETH Zurich. He has been professor at the Studio Basel of ETH Zurich since 1999, with Jacques Herzog, Pierre de Meuron and Roger Diener.

Peter Märkli completed his studies at ETH Zurich in 1977 and in the following year opened his own practice in Zurich. He has been a visiting professor in architectural design at ETH Zurich and EPF Lausanne and in 2002 he was appointed professor at ETH Zurich. In 2002 he was awarded the Heinrich-Tessenow Medal for his work.

Miller & Maranta Quintus Miller graduated in architecture from ETH Zurich in 1987. From 1990 to 1994 he was an assistant at the EPF Lausanne and ETH Zurich. Since 1994 Miller has collaborated in partnership with Paola Maranta in Basel. In 2000 he was visiting professor at EPF Lausanne. Paola Maranta studied architecture at EPF Lausanne and graduated from ETH Zurich in 1986. In 1990 she completed a Master of Business Administration at the IMD in Lausanne. From 1991 to 1994 she was a management consultant in Zurich and in 2000 visiting professor at EPF Lausanne.

Morger & Degelo Architekten Meinrad Morger was born in 1957. After an apprenticeship as a draughtsman he studied architecture at the HTL Winterthur and at ETH Zurich. He has been both assistant and visiting professor at ETH Zurich as well as visiting professor at EPF Lausanne. Heinrich Degelo, born in 1957, was apprenticed as a furniture joiner and as a draughtsman. He studied interior design and product design at the design school (Schule für Gestaltung) in Basel and continued his studies in the USA and Mexico. Between 1984 and 1986 Degelo worked for Herzog & de Meuron. Morger and Degelo started their own practice in Basel in 1988. They have received various prizes, among them the Balthasar-Neumann-Preis. In 2002 Benjamin Theiler, a graduate of ETH Zurich, became a partner.

Valerio Olgiati graduated from ETH Zurich in 1986 and then worked there as assistant to Professor Fabio Reinhart. From 1993 to 1995 he worked in the practice of Frank Escher in Los Angeles. In 1994 Olgiati was visiting lecturer at the Hochschule für Technik in Stuttgart and two years later he started his own practice in Zurich. Between 1998 and 2000 he was visiting lecturer at ETH Zurich. He also taught at the Accademia di architettura in Mendrisio and at the Architectural Association, London.

After finishing an apprenticeship as a carpenter Peter Zumthor studied at the design school (Schule für Gestaltung) in Basel, graduating in 1963. Thereafter he studied at the Pratt Institute in New York until 1966. From 1968 to 1978 he was an architect in the Department for the Preservation of Monuments in Graubünden. He started his own practice in 1979 in Haldenstein. He has taught widely, including in the USA, Germany and Switzerland. He is currently professor at the Accademia di architettura in Mendrisio. Zumthor has received international prizes and honours for his work, which has been exhibited in numerous architectural galleries, museums and architecture schools, including ETH Zurich, the Architectural Association London and the Biennale in Venice.

Project credits

Bearth + Deplazes

Chairlift Station, Arosa, Graubünden
Realization: June 2000–December 2000 / Architects: Bearth + Deplazes Architekten AG, Chur / Project director: Daniel Ladner / Builders: Arosa Bergbahnen, Arosa / Building engineers: Fredy Unger, Chur / Construction of chairlift: Garaventa AG

House Meuli, Fläsch, Graubünden
Realization: August 2000–May 2001 / Commission: Claudia and Andrea Meuli, Fläsch / Project architect: Claudia Drilling / Project supervision: Bearth + Deplazes Architekten AG, Chur / Engineers: Conzett, Bronzini, Gartmann AG, Chur / Physics: Edy Toscano AG, Chur

Ice-rink conversion, Arosa, Graubünden
Competition: 2000–2001 / Reworking of the competition entry: March 2002 / Collaborators: Pascal Hunkeler, Marlene Wallimann, Hitsch Largiadèr / Cost planning: Walter Dietsche, Chur / Technical installation: Grünberg + Partner AG, Zurich / Façade: Tuchschmid AG, Frauenfeld

Contemporary Art Gallery, Marktoberdorf, Germany
Realization: November 1999 – March 2001 / Commission: Kunst- und Kulturstiftung Dr Geiger Haus, Marktoberdorf / Project architect: Bettina Werner / Project supervision: Stephan Walter, architect, Kempten / Engineers: Jürg Buchli, Haldenstein / Physics: Edy Toscano AG, Chur

Burkhalter Sumi Architekten

EMPA renovation, Dübendorf, Zurich
Competition: 1995, First prize / Realization: 2002 / Commission: Bauten Forschungsanstalten Dübendorf, formerly Amt für Bundesbauten, Zurich / Collaborators: Jürg Schmid, Volker Lubnow, Hermann Kohler / Supervision: Burkhalter Sumi Architekten GmbH, represented by GMS Partner AG, Zurich / Engineers: Zimmermann + Volkert, Dübendorf, SHNZ Cham / Landscape design: Vogt Landschaftsarchitekten AG, Zurich

Multi-Family Villas, Witikon, Zurich
Competition: 1998, First prize / Realization: 2002 / Commission: Brigit Wehrli, Rosmarie Flüeler, Zurich / Commission representative: Immopro, Zurich / Collaborators: Yves Schihin, Michael Mettler, Elena Fernandez, Jürg Schmid, Benedikt Sunder-Plassmann / Contractor: Halter GU, Zurich / Supervision: ARGE Eckert + Lanz Bauleitungen, Zurich / Engineers: Hauser und Gebert, Fällanden / Landscape design: Vogt Landschafts-architekten AG, Zurich

Office Centre, Opfikon, Zurich
Competition: 2000, First prize / Realization: 2001 / Commission: HRS Generalunternehmer, Kreuzlingen / Consultants: Wüest + Partner, Zurich / Collaborators: Jürg Schmid, Katharina Mannhart / Engineers: Ribi und Blum, Kreuzlingen / Thermal engineers: Amstein Walthert, Zurich / Façades: Mebatech AG, Baden / Landscape design: Vogt Landschaftsarchitekten, Zurich

Sulzer Building renovation, Winterthur
Realization: 2001 / Commission: Sulzer Immobilien AG, Winterthur / Collaborators: Frank Imhof, Katharina Mannhart / Supervision: Burkhalter Sumi Architekten GmbH, represented by Axima FM AG, Winterthur / Engineers: Axima FM AG, Winterthur / Landscape design: Vogt Landschaftsarchitekten AG, Zurich / Interiors: vitra.point, a.spring ag, Zurich / Lighting design consultant: Christian Vogt, Winterthur

Gion A. Caminada

Stalls and Abattoir, Vrin, Graubünden
Realization: 1999 / Commission: Genossenschaft Mazlaria, Vrin / Collaborators: Thomas Stettler, Toni Pfister / Engineers: Fanchini + Pèrez

Totenstube, Vrin, Graubünden
Realization: 2002 / Commission: Gemeinde Vrin /

Collaborators: Thomas Stettler, Francesco Forcella / Engineers: Conzett, Bronzini, Gartmann AG, Chur

Single-family house, Vignon, Graubünden
Realization: 2000 / Commission: Karl Segmüller, Vignon / Collaborators: Thomas Stettler / Engineers: Conzett, Bronzini, Gartmann AG, Chur

Hotel Alpina, Vals, Graubünden
Realization: 2001 / Commission: Ursi and Karl Kühne, Vals / Collaborators: Gianluca De Pedrini / Engineers: Kilchmann Alex Schluein

Jürg Conzett

Surasuns Footbridge, Viamala, Graubünden
Competition: 1997 / Realization: 1999 / Commission: KulturRaum Viamala, Sils i. Domleschg / Montage: Valentin Luzi Bauunternehmung, Zillis / Anchors: Otto Bohr AG, Thusis / Steelworks: Romei AG Edelstahlverarbeitung Isla, Rothenbrunnen / Pavement: Granitwerk Andeer, Conrad A. AG, Andeer / Air transport: Air Grischa, Heliswiss Graubünden, Untervaz

Pedestrian Bridge, Bruges, Belgium
Realization: 2001 – 2002 / Commission: Ministerie van de Vlaamse Gemeenschap Afedeling Waterwegen Kust, Oostende / Contractor: Depret NV, Zeebrugge / Mechanical engineers: Jürg Meier, Niederurnen / Motor: Boekholt Transmissions, Wommelgem / Pipe: Metaalconstructie Aelterman b.v.b.a., Ghent / Pavement: Moderne Schrijnwerkerij Gebroeders Holvoet, Izegem Lighting design: Mosersidler AG für Lichtplanung, Zurich

Footbridge, Viamala, Graubünden
Still in planning phase

Diener & Diener

Jave Island housing, Amsterdam, the Netherlands
Competition: May 1995 / Realization: July 1999 – June 2001 / Participants in the competition: Uytenhaak, the Netherlands; MBM (Martorell, Bohigas, Mackay), Barcelona, Spain; Snozzi, Switzerland; Diener & Diener, Switzerland / Commission: Commune Amsterdam / Constructor: Amstelland Vastgoed BV, Amsterdam / Contractor: Koopmans Bouwgroup BV, Enschede

ABB Power Tower, Baden
Competition: November 1999 / Realization: October 2001 – November 2002 / Builder: ABB Immobilien AG, Baden / User: ABB Utility Automation AG, ALSTOM Switzerland Ltd / Urban planning: Zulauf & Partner, Baden / Metron / Landscape design: Landschaftsplanung AG, Bruges / Engineers: Ernst Basler & Partner AG, Zurich, Proplaning AG, Basel

Commercial centre, Lucerne
Competition: June 1995 / Realization: 1998 – 2000 / Commission: Genossenschaft Migros, Lucerne, Hotel Schweizerhof AG, Lucerne / Supervision: TGS Partner Architekten, Lucerne / Cost planning: Büro für Bauökonomie, Lucerne / Landscape design: Stefan Koepfli, Lucerne

Swiss Embassy, Berlin, Germany
Competition: 1995 / Realization: 1998 – 2000 / Commission: Federal Department of Finance / Coordination Office of Construction and Civil Engineering, Office of Federal Buildings, Buildings Abroad / Federal Office of Buildings and Logistics / West façade relief: Helmut Federle, artist / Landscape design: Kienast, Vogt + Partners, landscape architects, Zurich / Engineers: Walther Mory Maier Bauingenieure AG, Basel / Concrete consultant: Consultant Béton Architectonique, J. P. Aury, Paris / Art: Pippilotti Rist

Gigon & Guyer

Liner Museum, Appenzell
Planning / realization: September 1996 – September 1998 / Commission: Stiftung Carl Liner Vater und Sohn / Collaborators: Urs Birchmeier (project supervision), Daniel Kaufmann (supervision), Chantal Imoberdorf (P) /

Graphic designer: Trix Wetter, Zurich / Engineers: Aerni + Aerni, Zurich

Susenbergstrasse apartment buildings, Zurich
Competition: August 1998, First prize / Planning and realization: September 1998 – October/November 2000 / Commission: Zürcher Frauenverein (ZFV), represented by Rosemarie Michel / Collaborators: Peter Steiner (supervision), Samuel Thoma, Roger Naegeli (P) / Competition: Michael Widrig, Chantal Imoberdorf (P), Stefan Thommen (P) / Management and supervision: GU Göhner Merkur AG / Colours (realization): Adrian Schiess, Mouans-Sartoux, France / Colours (competition stage): Gigon & Guyer / Engineers: Dr Lüchinger + Meyer, Zurich / Landscape design: Zulauf, Seippel, Schweingruber, Baden / Constructors: K. Eicher AG, Regensdorf

Kalkriese Archaeological Museum Park, Osnabrück, Germany
Competition: July 1998 / Planning and realization: 1999 – 2002 / Commission: Varusschlacht im Osnabrücker Land Museum und Park Kalkriese / Collaborators: Planning: Volker Mencke (project architect), Massimo Wüthrich, Christian Brunner, Christoph Loetscher (P), Pieter Rabijns (P), Sebastian Thaut (P), Esther Hodel (P) / Competition: Markus Lüscher, Caspar Oswald (P) / Landscape design: Zulauf, Seippel, Schweingruber, Baden Lukas Schweingruber (landscape supervision), Heimer + Herbstreit, Hildesheim (costs, landscape supervision) / Exhibition design: integral concept, Ruedi Bauer, Lars Müller, Paris/Baden / Collaborators: Axel Steinberger (supervision) / Cost supervision: pbr Büro Rohling, Osnabrück, Hubert Conrady (project management), Daniela Wilker (supervision) / Engineers: Gantert + Wiemeler Ingenieurplanung, Münster

Pflegiareal housing and offices, Zurich
Research commission: September 1998 – February 1999, First prize / New buildings: Planning March 1999 onwards, realization November 2000 – November 2002 / Existing buildings: Planning March 1999 onwards, realization March 2000 – December 2000 / Commission: Stiftung

Diakoniewerk Neumünster – Schweizerische Pflegerinnenschule, Zurich / Collaborators: (competition) Gaby Kägi, Pascal Müller / New buildings (planning): Christian Maggioni (project supervision), Gaby Kägi, Philippe Vaucher, Ivo Lenherr, Arnault Biou, Andrea Fiechter / New buildings (realization): Koni Witzig, Micha Wiher, Peter Steiner / Existing buildings (planning): Christian Maggioni (project supervision), Eva Geering / Existing buildings (realization): Peter Steiner, Andrea Fiechter / Landscape design: Zulauf, Seippel, Schweingruber, Baden / Collaborators: Christoph Schubert / Engineers: Basler & Hofmann, Zurich / Colours: (competition) Gigon & Guyer (realization) Adrian Schiess, Mouans-Sartoux, France

Marcel Meili, Markus Peter Architekten
(Marcel Meili, Markus Peter, Zeno Vogel, Tobias Wieser)

RiffRaff 2, Zurich
Realization: 1999 – 2002 / Commission: Neugass Kino AG (cinema + bistro RiffRaff), Lifä AG (apartments) / Collaborators: Astrid Staufer & Thomas Hasler, Frauenfeld and Zurich / Project architect: Milan Augustin / Construction supervision: Urs Jörger, Gianesi & Hofmann, Zumikon / Engineers: Karl Dillier, Seuzach / Acoustics, mechanical engineers: Andi Mühlebach, Wiesendangen

Swiss Re Rüschlikon Centre for Global Dialogue, Zurich
Realization: 1995 – 2000 / Commission: Swiss Re, Switzerland / Project supervision: Tobias Wieser, Detlef Schulz / Collaborators: Martin Aerne, Maria Åström, Aita Flury, Samuel Gäumann, Carole Iselin, Adrian Kast, Nadja Keller, Christian Penzel, Patrick Sidler, Jürg Spaar, Katharina Stehrenberger, Othmar Villiger, Adrian Weber / Project management/supervision: Karl Steiner AG, Zurich / Landscape design: Kienast Vogt Partner, Zurich / Interiors: Hermann Czech, architect, Vienna, Adolf Krischanitz, architect, Vienna / Textile art: Gilbert Bretterbauer, Vienna / Art project villa: Günther Förg, Areuse / Engineers: Fietz AG Bauingenieure, Zurich Conzett, Bronzini, Gartmann AG, Chur

Parasite House, Rotterdam, the Netherlands
Realization: 2001–2002 / Commission: Vestia Hoogvliet
and Parasite Foundation / Project management: Mechthild
Stuhlmacher / Project supervision: Adrian Weber /
Collaborators: Andreas Schmidt / Timber construction:
Schilliger Holz AG, Küssnacht, Haltikon, Blumer-Lehmann
AG, Gossau/Erlenhof / Colours: Bau + Kunst, Tashi
Lindegger, Attikon

Swiss Embassy, Washington, DC, USA
Research project: 2001 / Commission: Eidgenössisches
Department des Äusseren / Collaborators: Sabine
Harmuth, Christina Ringelmann / Engineers: Conzett,
Bronzini, Gartmann AG, Chur / Landscape design: Vogt
Landschaftsarchitekten, Zurich / Collaborators: Rita Illien

Peter Märkli

La Congiunta, Giornico, Ticino
Realization: 1992 / Collaborators: Stefan Bellwalder,
Naters

Single-family house, Hünenberg
Realization: 2000 / Collaborators: Gody Kühnis, Trübbach /
Landscape design: Rotzler Krebs Partner GmbH,
Winterthur

School, Zurich North
Realization: 2001 / Project supervision: Jacob
Frischknecht, Christof Ansorge, Zurich, in collaboration
with Gody Kühnis, Trübbach / Landscape architecture:
Zulauf, Seippel, Schweingruber, Baden

Single-family house, Azmoos
Realization: 2000 / Collaborators: Gody Kühnis, Trübbach

Miller & Maranta

Market hall, Aarau
Competition: April 1996 / Realization: November
2001 – August 2002 / Commission: Commune of the city
of Aarau / Collaborators: Peter Baumberger, Sabine

Rosenthaler / Engineers: Conzett, Bronzini,
Gartmann AG, Chur

Schwarzpark apartments, Basel
Competition: 2001 / Realization: November 2002 – August
2004 / Commission: Zentralstelle für staatlichen
Liegenschaftsverkehr, Basel/Hochbau- und Planungsamt,
Basel / Collaborators: Peter Baumberger, Ines Siegrist /
Engineers: Conzett, Bronzini, Gartmann AG, Chur

Volta Schoolhouse, Basel
Competition: November 1996 / Realization: 1998 – 2000 /
Commission: Construction Department Kanton Basel-
Stadt / Collaborators: Othmar Brügger, Peter Baumberger,
Michael Meier, Marius Hug / Engineers: Conzett,
Bronzini, Gartmann AG, Chur (project), Affentrager +
Partner AG (realization) / Landscape design: August
Künzel, Binningen / Art: Erik Steinbrecher, Berlin / Graphic
design: Susanna Stammbach, Basel

Morger & Degelo Architekten
(Partners: Meinrad Morger, Heinrich Degelo,
Benjamin Theiler)

Liechtenstein Art Museum, Vaduz
Competition: 1997, Second prize / Planning: 1998 /
Realization: 1999 – 2000 / Commission: Stiftung zur
Errichtung eines Kunstmuseums Liechtenstein /
Collaborators: Nicole Woog, Heike Buchmann,
Dagmar Strasser, Raeto Studer / Engineers: Josef
Schwartz, Oberägeri

St. Alban-Ring housing, Basel
Competition: 1999, First prize / Project/realization:
2000 – 2002 / Commission: Pensimo Management AG,
Zurich / Collaborators: Dagmar Strasser, André Buess /
Engineers: Burger & Partner, Basel

House Müller, Staufen, Basel

Project commission: 1998 / Realization: 1999 /
Commission: Mrs V. Müller, Lenzburg / Collaborators:
Romana Tedeschi / Engineers: WGG Ingenieure
SIA/ASIC, Basel

Reinach town centre, Basel

Competition: 1997, first prize / Planning: 1998 – 1999 /
Realization: 2000 – 2002 / Commission: Community
Reinach / Pensimo Management AG, Zurich /
Collaborators: Marianne Kempf, Raeto Studer, Stefan
Frehner, Cristina de Marchi, Franziska Felber, Nicola
Senn / Engineers: Affentrager + Partner Bauingenieure
AG, Basel, WGG Ingenieure SIA/ASIC, Basel

Valerio Olgiati

Schoolhouse, Paspels, Graubünden

Competition: July 1996 / Realization: March 1997 – April
1998 / Commission: Community of Paspels / Planning:
Iris Dätwyler, Gaudenz Zindel, Raphael Zuber /
Construction supervision: Peter Diggelmann / Engineers:
Gebhard Decasper

Yellow House, Flims, Graubünden

Realization: October 1998 – October 1999 / Commission:
Community of Flims / Planning: Iris Dätwyler, Pascal
Flammer, Karen Wassung, Raphael Zuber / Construction
supervision: Walter Carigi, Peter Diggelmann /
Engineers: Conzett, Bronzini, Gartmann AG, Chur

Office building, Zurich

Competition: June 2001, First prize / Commission:
Neues Warenhaus AG / Planning: Theo Barmettler,
Pascal Flammer, Eva-Maria Stadelmann

Peter Zumthor

Sound Box, Hanover Expo 2000, Germany

Realization: 2000 / Architect and artistic director: Peter
Zumthor / Project architect: Rainer Weitschies / Project
team: Daniel Bosshard (competition), Uta J. Graff, Kirsi

Leiman / Construction supervision: Franz Bärtsch /
Structural engineer: Jürg Conzett / Curator of sound and
music: Daniel Ott / Word curator: Plinio Bachmann /
Supervision of catering provision: Max Rigendinger /
Direction and mise-en-scène: Karoline Gruber /
Wardrobe mistress: Ida Gut

Topography of Terror, Berlin, Germany

Realization: 1993 – 2005 / Project architect: Rainer
Weitschies / Structural engineers: Jürg Buchli and
Herbert Fink / Mechanical engineering: Meierhans
and Partners

Single-family house, Graubünden

Realization: 1997 – 2003 / Project architect: Michael Hemmi

Kunsthaus Bregenz, Austria

Realization: 1990 – 1997 / Project architect (museum
building): Daniel Bosshard / Project architect (administra-
tion building): Thomas Kämpfer / Project team: Jürg
Bumann, Roswitha Büsser, Katja Dambacher, Thomas
Durisch, Marlene Gujan / Structural engineer: Robert
Manahl / Construction supervision: Siegfried Wäger,
Martin Zerlauth / Mechanical engineering: Meierhans and
Partner / Daylight engineering: Hanns Freymuth

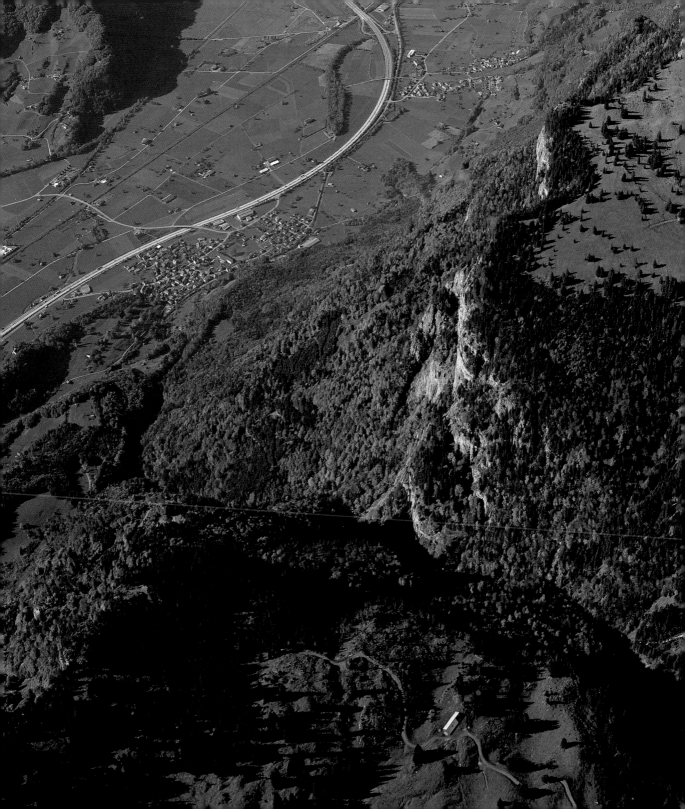

Bibliography

Gion A. Caminada, *Stiva da morts. Vom Nutzen der Architektur (House of Rest. The Uses of Architecture)* (Zurich: GTA Verlag, 2003).

Jürg Conzett, Mohsen Mostafavi, Andreas Hagmann, Bruno Reichlin, *Structure as Space: Engineering and Architecture in the Works of Jürg Conzett* (London: Architectural Association, 2003).

Tibor Joanelly, 'Wahrenbachhalde housing', *Werk, Bauen & Wohnen*, vol.89/56, no.12, Dec 2002.

Tibor Joanelly, Michael Hauser, Ernst Hubeli and Marcel Meili in conversation with Tibor Joanelly, 'Housing with Cinema and RiffRaff Bistro', *Werk, Bauen & Wohnen*, vol.89/56, no.12, Dec, 2002.

Pamela Johnston (ed.), *Marcel Meili, Markus Peter Architects, Zurich: The House of Stone* (London: Architectural Association, 2002).

Mohsen Mostafavi (ed.), *Approximations: The Architecture of Peter Märkli* (London: Architectural Association, 2002).

'Valerio Olgiati' (incl. Kenneth Frampton, 'Olgiati's Almost Nothing'), *A+U*, no.4 (379), Apr 2002.

Andre Bideau, 'A Full Urban Neighbourhood: A Repair of the Urban Landscape by Miller & Maranta', *Werk, Bauen & Wohnen*, special issue: 'Tiefe Oberflächen' ('Deep Surfaces'), vol.88/55, no.3, Mar 2001.

Andrea Deplazes, 'Wood: Indifferent, Synthetic, Abstract – Man-made', *Werk, Bauen & Wohnen*, vol.88/55, no.1/2, Jan/Feb 2001.

Jacques Lucan, *Matière d'Art/A Matter of Art: Contemporary Architecture in Switzerland* (Basel: Birkhäuser, 2001).

Susanne Muller, 'Brücken in der Viamala' ('Bridges in the Viamala'), *Topos*, special issue: 'Eingriffe' ('Interventions'), no.36, Sept, 2001.

Roberto Petruzzi, 'Peter Zumthor: Tre Opera', ('Peter Zumthor: Three Works'), *Parametro*, vol.31, no.233, Mar/Apr, 2001.

Vicky Richardson, *New Vernacular Architecture* (London: King, 2001).

Elisabeth von Samsonow, *Swiss Re Rüschlikon. Centre for Global Dialogue*, Kunsthaus Bregenz, Archiv Kunst Architektur, Werkdokumente 20 (Ostfildern-Ruit: Hatje Cantz, 2001).

Steven Spier, 'Place, Authorship and the Concrete: Three Conversations with Peter Zumthor', *Architectural Research Quarterly*, CUP, vol.5, no.1, 2001.

Christoph Wieser, 'Carmenna chair lift building, Arosa', *Werk, Bauen & Wohnen*, special issue: 'Massgeschneidert' ('Made to Measure'), vol.88/55, no.4, April 2001.

'Vertrauensbildende Zeitlosigkeit – Gedanken zur Innenraumgestaltung des Centre for Global Dialogue' ('Classic Furnishings – Thoughts on the Interior Design of the Centre for Global Dialogue'), *Werk, Bauen & Wohnen*, vol.88/55, no.7/8, July/Aug 2001.

'Werk-Material. Voltaschulhaus Basel' ('Volta School in Basel'), *Werk, Bauen & Wohnen*, vol.88/55, no. 3, Mar 2001.

Christoph Bürkle (ed.), *Gigon/Guyer Architects: Works & Projects 1989 – 2000* (Sulgen: Niggli, 2000).

Christoph Bürkle, *Morger & Degelo Architekten* (Sulgen: Niggli, 2000).

Christoph Bürkle, 'Rhetorik des Rationalen' ('Rhetoric of the Rational'), *Archithese*, vol.30, no.3, May/June 2000.

Jürg Conzett, 'Jürg Conzett & Partners: Two Bridges', *AA Files*, no.41, summer 2000.

Annette Gigon, Mike Guyer (eds Brian Carter and Annette W. LeCuyer), 'Gigon/Guyer', The 2000 Charles & Ray Eames Lecture (Ann Arbor, Mich: A. Alfred Taubman College of Architecture and Urban Planning, University of Michigan, 2000).

Annette Gigon, Mike Guyer (eds Kunsthaus Bregenz, Archiv Kunst Architektur, Edelbert Kob), *Gigon & Guyer: Museum Liner Appenzell* (Ostfildern-Ruit: Hatje Cantz, 2000).

Christian Kerez, Stiftung zur Errichtung eines Kunstmuseums Vaduz/Liechtenstein (ed.), *Kunstmuseum Liechtenstein: Morger Degelo Kerez Architekten (Art Museum Liechtenstein)* (Baden: Müller, 2000).

Kunsthaus Bregenz, Archiv Kunst Architektur, Edelbert Köb (eds), *Das Gelbe Haus (The Yellow House)* (Ostfildern-Ruit: Hatje Cantz, 2000).

Marcel Meili, *Schweizerische Hochschule für die Holzwirtschaft, Biel: Marcel Meili, Markus Peter mit Zeno Vogel* (Swiss School of Engineering for the Wood Industry, Biel) (Sulgen, Zurich: Niggli, 2000).

Ulrich Müller, *Stadt Haus Architektur (City, House, Architecture)*, Architektur Galerie Leipzig (Berlin: Mann, 2000).

Charles Rattray, Graeme Hutton, 'Concepts and Material Associations in the Work of Gigon Guyer', *ARQ: Architectural Research Quarterly*, vol.4, no.1, 2000.

Cordula Seger, 'School in Paspels', *Baumeister*, special issue: 'Konzepte. Entwerfen zwischen Intuition und Vernunft, Zufall und Kalkul' ('Concept. Designing Between Intuition and Reason, Chance and Calculation'), vol.97, no.1, Jan 2000.

Cyrille Simonnet, 'La passerelle Surasuns, Viamala, Coira, Suisse' ('The Surasuns Footbridge, Viamala, Chur, Switzerland'), *Architecture d'Aujourd'hui*, no. 329, July/ Aug 2000.

Martin Tschanz, 'Valerio Olgiati: Works', *AA Files*, no.42, autumn 2000.

Heinz Wirz (ed.), *14 Studentenprojekte bei Valerio Olgiati 1998 – 2000* ('Valerio Olgiati: 14 Student Projects 1998 – 2000') (Lucerne: Quart, 2000).

Peter Zumthor, Plinio Bachmann et al., *Klangkörperbuch: Lexikon zum Pavillon der Schweizerischen Eidgenossenschaft an der Expo 2000 in Hannover* ('The Sound Box Book: Lexicon of the Pavilion of the Swiss Federation at Expo 2000 in Hanover') (Basel: Birkhäuser 2000).

'Baumaterial – der Stoff, aus dem die Räume sind' ('Building Materials'), vol.97, Sept 2000.

El Croquis, special issue: 'Annette Gigon and Mike Guyer 1989 – 2000', no.4 (102), 2000.

'School, Duvin', *2G*, special issue: 'Construir en las montanas. Arquitectural reciente en los Grisones' ('Building in the Mountains. Recent Architecture in Graubünden'), no.14 (2), 2000.

Hubertus Adam, *Morger & Degelo: Haus Müller in Staufen, 1998 – 99 (Morger & Degelo: Müller House in Staufen)* (Zurich: GTA Verlag, 1999).

Valentin Bearth, Andrea Deplazes, *Räumlinge* (Lucerne: Quart, 1999); *Spacepieces* (English ed., 2000).

Philipp Esch, 'Eigene Angelegenheiten' (Mursteg Bridge, Murau, Austria), *Archithese*, vol.29, no.5, Sept/Oct 1999.

Mohsen Mostafavi, 'The Swiss School of Engineering for the Wood Industry, Biel', *AA Files*, no.39, 1999.

Lynnette Widder, Steven Spier, Eugene Asse and Detlef Mertins, *Burkhalter & Sumi* (Basel: Birkhäuser, 1999).

'Miller & Maranta', *Junge Basler Architekturbüros (Young Basel Architecture Practices)* (Basel: Architektur-museum, 1999).

Christoph Allenspach, *Architektur in der Schweiz: Bauen im 19. und 20. Jahrhundert* (Zurich: Pro Helvetia, 1998).

Alberto Dell'Antonio, *Paspels: Valerio Olgiati* (Zurich: Simonett, 1998).

Martin Kieren, Christian Vogt, *Diener & Diener Architekten: Bauten und Entwürfe 1981 – 1996 (Diener & Diener Architects: Buildings and Proposals 1981 – 96)* (Basel: Birkhäuser, 1998).

Vittorio Magnago Lampugnani and Martin Steinmann, *Stadtansichten: Diener & Diener (City Views. Diener & Diener)* (Zurich: GTA Verlag, 1998).

Christoph Luchsinger, 'School in Vella', *Werk, Bauen & Wohnen*, special issue: 'Technische Architektur – Abschied vom Pathos' ('Technical Architecture – Farewell to Emotionalism)', no.1/2, Jan/Feb 1998.

Anna Meseure, Martin Tschanz and Wilfried Wang, *Schweiz* (Munich: Prestel, 1998).

Martin Steinmann, 'You See What You See: A House by Peter Märkli in Ehrlenbach', *Archithese*, vol.28, no.1, Jan/Feb 1998.

Charles Tashima, 'Three Urban Pieces: Recent Collaborative Work by Meili & Peter Architects', *AA Files*, no.36, 1998.

Peter Zumthor, *Peter Zumthor Works: Buildings and Projects 1979 – 97*, photographs by Hélène Binet (Baden: Müller, 1998).

Peter Zumthor, *Thinking Architecture* (Baden: Müller, 1998).

Christoph Bürkle and Architektur Forum Zürich, *Junge Schweizer Architekte/Young Swiss Architects* (Sulgen: Niggli, 1997).

Jürg Conzett, 'Containing space', *Werk, Bauen & Wohnen*, special issue: 'Ingenieur formt mit' ('The Engineer as Co-Designer'), no.9, 1997.

Mercedes Daguerre, *Architekturführer Schweiz: 20. Jahrhundert* (Basel: Birkhäuser, 1997).

Manfred Sack, Peter Zumthor, *Three Concepts: Thermal Baths Vals, Art Museum Bregenz, 'Topography of Terror'*, catalogue of an exhibition in Architekturgalerie Luzern (Basel: Birkhäuser, 1997).

Ulrike Jehle-Sculte Strathaus, 'Giovani studi di architettura di Basilea' ('Young Architectural Partnerships in Basel), *Domus*, no.795, July/Aug 1997.

'Marianne Burkhalter and Christian Sumi', *AA Files*, no.34, 1997.

'Schulhaus in Duvin' ('School in Duvin'), *Werk, Bauen & Wohnen*, no.7/8, July/Aug 1997.

'Stallneubau, Vrin GR' ('New Stable Building'), *Werk, Bauen & Wohnen*, no.12, Dec 1997.

Max Bill, *Minimal Tradition: Max Bill und die 'einfache Architektur 1942 – 1996'* (Baden: Müller, 1996).

Marianne Burkhalter and Christian Sumi, *Die Holzbauten* ('Timber Buildings') (Zurich: GTA Verlag, 1996).

Peter Zumthor, *The Thermal Bath at Vals* (London: Architectural Association, 1996).

Roger Diener, Martin Steinmann, *Das Haus und die Stadt: Diener & Diener. Städtebauliche Arbeiten (The House and the City: Diener & Diener. Urban Studies)* (Basel: Birkhäuser, 1995).

Carmen Humbel, *Junge Schweizer Architekten und Architektinnen* ('Young Swiss Architects') (Zurich: Artemis, 1995).

Lynnette Widder, 'Positive Indifference', interview with Christian Sumi, *Daidalos*, special issue: 'Magic of Materials', Aug 1995.

'School in Malix', *Werk, Bauen & Wohnen*, 'Einzelfälle: Neue Beispiele aus dem Schweizer Architekturschaffen' ('Individual Cases: New Examples of Swiss Architecture'), no.5, May 1995.

Mark Gilbert and Kevin Alter (eds), *Construction, Intention, Detail: Five Projects from Five Swiss Architects/Fünf Projekte von fünf Schweizer Architekten* (Zurich: Artemis, 1994).

Kunsthaus Bregenz, Archiv Kunst Architektur, Edelbert Köb (eds), *Stiftung La Congiunta. Peter Märkli: Haus für Reliefs und Halbfiguren des Bildhauers Hans Josephsohn (La Congiunta Foundation. Peter Märkli: A House for Reliefs and Half Figures by the Sculptor Hans Josephson)* (Stuttgart: Hatje, 1994).

Rosamund Diamond, Winfried Wang (eds), *From City to Detail: Selected Buildings and Projects by Diener & Diener Architekten* (London: The Architecture Foundation, 1992).

Photography credits:

All photographs by Christian Richters unless listed below.

© Hans Ruedi Disch: p.10, top right
© Heinrich Helfenstein: p.11, below left; p.238, below right
© Rien Korteknie: pp.148–51
© Luftbild Schweiz: pp.1–3, 251
© A Moravansky: p.239, left below
© Steven Spier: p.10, top middle and below middle; p.11, middle and below right
© Martin Tschanz: p.238, all except below right; p.239, below middle and right
Courtesy of Archithese: p.239, right column, middle picture
Courtesy of Archivio Mario Botta, photograph by Adriano Heitmann: p.10, left column, middle picture
Courtesy of Reto Gort: p.26, below
Courtesy of Miller & Maranta, © Ruedi Walti: pp.172–77, 180–86
Courtesy of Valerio Olgiati: p.214
Courtesy of Peter Zumthor: p.224
Photograph by Valeriy G. Petrushechkin: p.11, top right
Photograph by Paolo Roselli: p.11, left column, middle picture

Acknowledgments:

There are many people whose help in bringing this book to publication I should like to acknowledge. There are my editors Lucas Dietrich and Catherine Hall whom I thank for their patience and good humour. There is Catherine Slessor of *Architectural Review*, who suggested that I write this book. I could not have done so without the immense help of Ines Geisler. There are many others of course who have helped me directly or at least put up with me during the process and they know who they are.

My fondness for Switzerland has by now a long history, but I must mention Professor H. E. Kramel who gave me, along with so many other foreigners, a job teaching at ETH Zurich and thus allowed me to get to know Switzerland and its society at first hand. Lastly I want to thank the many people I met as a result of writing this book, with whom I formed or strengthened friendships.

Steven Spier, Glasgow

p. 1: Aerial view of Andermatt and Gemsstock in the canton of Uri, 2002.
pp. 2–3: Aerial view of Walenstadt, Walensee and the Churfirsten mountains in the canton of St. Gallen, 1998.
pp. 4–5: Herzog & de Meuron, Ricola Warehouse, Laufen, 1986–87.

First published in the United Kingdom in 2003 by Thames & Hudson Ltd, 181A High Holborn, London WC1V 7QX

www.thamesandhudson.com

First paperback edition 2008

British Library Cataloguing-in-Publication Data
A catalogue record for this book is available from the British Library
ISBN 978-0-500-28779-8

Printed and bound in China by Everbest Printing Co.
Designed by Laurent Benner / Alberto Balsalm / Reala
Typographic assistance: Laurenz Brunner